To our very
GOOD FRIENDS.
We love you
THE CUNNINGHAM'S

THE HOLY BIBLE

Places and Stories from the Old and New Testament

JG PRESS

TEXT
GIANNI GUADALUPI

Editorial project
Valeria Manferto De Fabianis

Editorial coordination
Laura Accomazzo
Giada Francia
Enrico Lavagno
Federica Romagnoli

Graphic design
Clara Zanotti

Graphic realization
Patrizia Balocco Lovisetti

Translation
Timoty Stroud

1 *The birth of the Virgin Mary, from a 16th-century antiphonary
in the collegiate church of Santa Maria Impruneta.*

2-3 *The* Creation of Adam, *by Michelangelo Buonarroti. Sistine
Chapel, the Vatican.*

4-5 *The* Annunciation, *by Leonardo da Vinci, oil on wood, circa
1475. Florence, Uffizi Gallery.*

CONTENTS

PREFACE   *PAGE* 6

THE OLD TESTAMENT   *PAGE*   10

CHAPTER 1
FROM ADAM TO NOAH   *PAGE*   12

CHAPTER 2
THE TOWER OF BABEL AND
THE SCATTERING OF THE PEOPLES   *PAGE*   36

CHAPTER 3
ABRAHAM, ESAU AND JACOB:
JOSEPH IN EGYPT   *PAGE*   50

CHAPTER 4
MOSES AND THE EXODUS   *PAGE*   82

CHAPTER 5
THE LAND OF MILK AND HONEY   *PAGE*   118

CHAPTER 6
KING SAUL AND DAVID   *PAGE*   138

CHAPTER 7
THE SPLENDOR OF SOLOMON   *PAGE*   154

CHAPTER 8
THE DIVIDED KINGDOM   *PAGE*   168

CHAPTER 9
FROM THE BABYLONIAN CAPTIVITY
TO THE MACCABEAN REVOLT   *PAGE*   186

THE NEW TESTAMENT   *PAGE*   202

CHAPTER 10
HEROD THE GREAT AND
THE BIRTH OF THE MESSIAH   *PAGE*   204

CHAPTER 11
THE PALESTINE OF JESUS   *PAGE*   232

INDEX   *PAGE*   298

PHOTOGRAPHIC CREDITS   *PAGE*   302

Published by
World Publications Group, Inc.
140 Laurel Street
East Bridgewater, MA 02333
www.wrldpub.com

© 2003 White Star S.p.A.
Via Candido Sassone, 24 - 13100 Vercelli, Italy
www.whitestar.it

ISBN 978-1-57215-484-1

2 3 4 5 6 14 13 12 11 10

Printed and bound in Indonesia

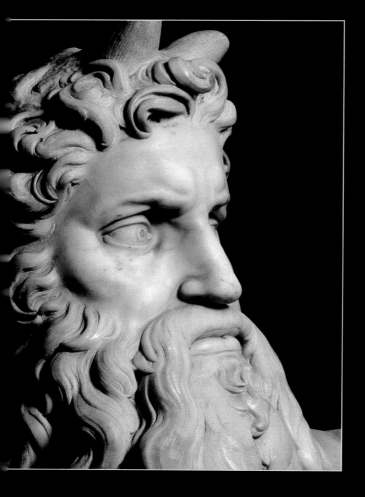

PREFACE

6 Moses, *by Michelangelo Buonarroti, circa 1515. This*
statue expresses the sorrow found in the master's
greatest works. Rome, San Pietro in Vincoli.

7 *The Jewish, Christian and Islamic faiths share the*
belief that Gebel Musa, in the Sinai, was where Moses
received the Ten Commandments from God.

Like medieval Christendom's *mappae mundi*, which adjusted the confusion of half-known geography to fit the requirements of theology, structuring and ranking the image of the world so that wise men could recognize God's designs in cartography, this book uses words and pictures to retrace the stories and places of the Bible. For believers, this holy story is the secret scheme that underlies the events of history. And like those medieval maps, this book is constructed in concentric circles. The outermost embrace Earthly Paradise, Noah's Mount Ararat, the Babylon of the arrogant Tower of Babel, and the Egypt of the Ten Plagues; the innermost ring encompasses the narrow strip of land known as Palestine, a country whose misfortune it is to have three religions interwoven in its history.

At the center, Jerusalem, the lynchpin of the Jewish and Christian world: the Temple and Holy Sepulcher, the Cross and the seven-branched candlestick. Moving like actors on a stage across this vast area – that includes much of the Near East, from the Nile to the Euphrates, from Eden to Golgotha – are the major and minor figures that have filled the collective imagination of the West for more than two thousand years. They include the Forefathers and the Patriarchs, the Prophets and the Apostles, Abraham and Isaac, Joseph and his brothers, Moses and the Ten Commandments, Joshua and the walls of Jericho, Samson and the Philistines, David and Goliath, Solomon the lover of the queen of Sheba, Jonah and the whale, and John the Baptist in the desert.

Over the centuries, an immense iconographic treasure has been created (and stylistically updated to match changing tastes) of the eternal and immortal stories of the Bible. With an impartial love for their artistic beauty, this book plays host to these works, from early Christian mosaics to Mannerist frescoes, from illuminations

8 *Mary leans her head toward the Child in* Rest during the Flight to Egypt, *painted in 1593 by Caravaggio. Rome, Galleria Doria Pamphilj.*

9 La Pietà, *by Giovanni Bellini, 1460, in the Pinacoteca di Brera, Milan. Here humanity is placed in dramatic confrontation with the divine.*

n Books of Hours to Symbolist and Pre-Raphaelite paintings.

Flanking the most famous – and minor or almost unknown – works of art, where it has been possible, this book includes modern photographs of the actual or presumed places where the events narrated took place. The comparison between imagination and reality, between a past that has become legendary and a present that is often unknown, is often surprising and always meaningful.

However, this is not, nor does it try to be, a book on biblical archaeology, nor a study of the bible stories that have been handed down to us, nor does it propose alternative sites for the various episodes in light of recent archaeological discoveries. It does no more than accept and report what the Bible says, corroborating and fleshing out stories where detail is often lacking with texts that might be defined as 'secondary.' The reader will therefore find stories from the Old and New Testaments,

supported by others found in books. These volumes are often less known or difficult to come by: for example, the invaluable *Antiquities of the Jews* by Flavius Josephus, and the writings of the many Christians who visited the Holy Land between the 4th century and the Crusades. These men and women saw the holy places of Jewish and Christian traditions that the construction of chapels, churches, basilicas and monasteries had monumentalized and legitimized.

Like the unquestioning accounts by those believers and credulous travelers, the pages of this book are filled with miracles and wonders, following the traces of a Chosen People before and after the coming of a Messiah. It provides another and itinerant look at the Bible, and an unusual, and, it is to be hoped, stimulating topographical interpretation of the Book of Books. It is a journey into the labyrinth of the sacred story, the thread of which is represented by God Himself.

THE OLD TESTAMENT

FROM **A**DAM TO NOAH

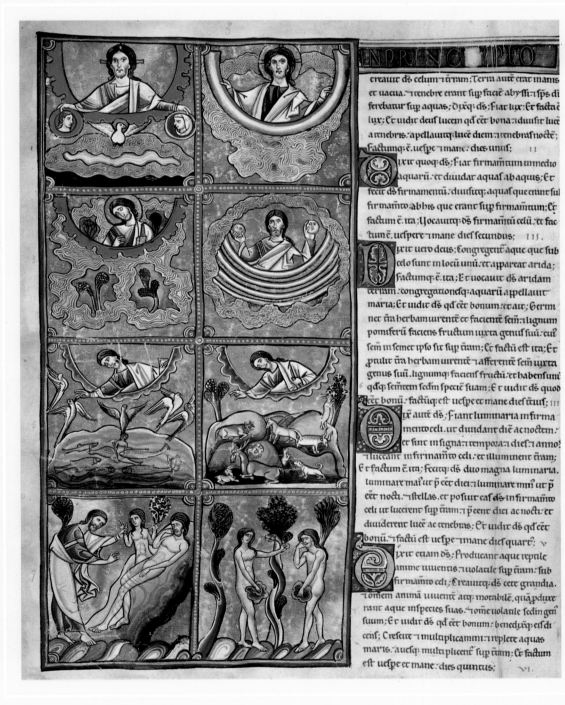

10-11 *This magnificent image in the Sistine Chapel's center vault shows the Creator's omnipotence as He brings plants and heavenly bodies into existence on the third and fourth days of the Creation.*

12 *God the Father measures the Cosmos. This illuminated page from the 12th-century* La Bible Moralisée *produced in Reims, France, presents the Creator as though he were simply an architect in the Gothic world, then at its height (National Library, Vienna).*

13 *Similar to a Byzantine Christ Pantokrator, God rules over the Creation. The image of* The Original Sin *concludes the series presented in the late 12th-century Souvigny Bible.*

The creation of the world

14 and 15 bottom *The* Creation *receives a Ptolemaic treatment in the* Liber Chronicarum (Chronicle of the World), *by Hartmann Schedel. Published in 1493, at a crucial moment in the transition between the Middle Ages and the modern era, this work is more famous for its 1,800 illustrations than for its contents. The images, printed from 645 wood engravings, present the six ages of the world, from the Creation to the birth of Christ.*

15 top *'It is not good that the man should be alone': God offered Adam help and company, first by creating animals and then with the creation of Eve. In this illustration from a copy of the Nuremberg Bible (1493), the first woman is formed from Adam's rib in the Garden of Eden. In Hebrew* eden *means 'delight' but it is interesting to note that originally the word meant 'partner.'*

Earthly paradise

 s the greatest of the religious orators of the 17th century, Jacques-Bénigne Bossuet, wrote in his *Discours sur l'histoire universelle* for the dauphin of France, "God must have said to himself that he had to make happy those beings that he had just created in his image and likeness." And thus Adam and Eve found themselves given a paradise to live in, i.e., a *paira-daèca*, the Persian word that means park, garden or place planted with trees. As Genesis tells us, God had adorned this paradise of Eden (i.e., paradise of delights) with every sort of tree and plant, beautiful to look at and with edible fruits. Two of these were particularly important: the Tree of Life, which was planted in the center of the garden, and the Tree of Knowledge or tree of good and evil, whose fruit

the couple were not allowed to eat. However, their disobedience, instigated by the serpent in which Satan concealed himself, had disastrous consequences.

Where was that Eden located? The Eden whose delights the first man and woman were unable to enjoy for long because, according to the Doctors of the Church, they sinned and were expelled the same day they were created. The Bible gives a fairly precise indication, saying that Eden was bathed by a river from which flowed four others: the Tigris, Euphrates, Pison and Gihon. We know the first two perfectly well but identification of the others has caused quarrels among commentators since Antiquity as it was impossible to recognize in them either the Nile or Indus, or even underground rivers, as the

16 In **The Garden of Eden** *by Hieronymus Bosch (early 16th century), the master's precise naturalistic depiction is merged with a visionary, surreal and symbolic approach only distantly related to the art of the period.*

16-17 In the work of the same title by Lucas Cranach (1530), the figures appear in the background in different episodes of the Book of Genesis. In keeping with biblical indications, Eden is situated on the Armenian plateau.

Banishment from the earthly paradise

more eager have proposed. More probable are the Kura and the Aras (Araxes), which join before flowing into the Caspian Sea. This hypothesis is geographically much more modest but less wildly imaginative. In any case, the location of the earthly paradise was somewhere on the Armenian plain, not far from Ararat, which was also to become an important biblical location, as we shall see.

Yet there are some who have wanted to set Eden in ancient Chaldea, closer to the Persian Gulf, where the weather was undoubtedly warmer than the Armenian climate, which was unfavorable to a garden of delights.

Another much debated question in past centuries was that of the language our two ancestors spoke during their short stay. "Hebrew, naturally," answered the Jews, but to non-Jews this reply seemed too simple, besides being veiled in nationalism, and each one attempted to argue for their own language. According to a Persian tradition, the serpent spoke Arabic, Adam and Eve conversed in exquisite literary Persian, and the Archangel Gabriel chased them out in Turkish. A three-language version was also put forward in the 17th century by the Swedish scholar Andrea Kempe but with a Nordic

twist: according to him, God spoke to Adam in Swedish and the first man replied in Danish. As for the serpent, it tempted Eve in French, the language of sin. The 18th century saw the popularity of Basque, which was thought, with some justification, to be the oldest language on earth. The chapter house in Pamplona cathedral contains a record of a detailed debate on the subject, concluding that though there was no proof in favor of it, there was none against it either, and restated the warmly held conviction that the language of Eden was Basque, probably in its Navarrine variant.

But whichever language the serpent spoke, from that moment it lost the power of speech as a divine punishment for its mellifluous words and the lies with which it had persuaded Eve to commit sin. As for the guilty couple, the woman would forever give birth in pain, and the man work with sweat on his brow, condemned, as one misogynist exegete put it, "because he had given heed to womanly wiles."

Not far from the paradisiacal garden from which they were expelled and into which none of their offspring could ever enter, Adam and Eve began their new lives.

Cain and Abel

The cradle of humanity was, therefore, Mesopotamia, a fertile land between two rivers where they raised sons and daughters. First, two males were born, Cain and Abel, whose rivalry resulted in fratricide. After committing his crime, cursed in the eyes of the Lord but untouchable, Cain wandered the world in remorse and ended up settling in a country called Nod, meaning "land of agitation and upheaval," because he lived there as an outcast tormented by his guilt. Nod lay "on the east of Eden" in a location that is too vague to allow identification, nor does it help us to know that he founded a city there called Enoch, after his first born, Enoch.

20 top In this Italian Renaissance painting, the young Cain, a future cultivator, follows his mother who carries her younger son, Abel, destined to be a herder, in her arms. The story of the two brothers may have had its origins in a clash between nomadic herders – like the tribes of Israel – and a settled farming community.

20 bottom In this illuminated capital letter, painted in the 15th century by Belbello of Pavia, Lamech, Cain's fourth-generation descendant, slays his forefather despite the prohibition by God.

20-21 In 1543 Titian painted a dark vision of the first murder in human history, which was caused by God's preference for Abel's offerings.

NOBILIS PATRIARCHARVM CETVS

The line of man

This first human settlement — which to us may seem the beginning of civilization — appears in the Bible to be treated with a shade of disapproval: it was a human work, not divine, and might even be termed anti-divine because it was the work of a man damned. Equally reprehensible because they were too human and too earthly were the innovations and inventions to which the descendants of Cain devoted themselves: Lamech introduced polygamy; Jabel "was the father of such as dwell in tents and of such as have cattle," i.e., nomads; Jubal made a harp and created music; Tubalcain was "instructor of every artificer in brass and iron"; and

the longevity of men at that time brought great advantages for Good, it unfortunately gave the wicked greater facility to give themselves up to their passions, and to corrupt the good with their bad example. Death, being very rare, did not strike down the sinners with its severe lesson, and the time left to them before they appeared before God increased their audacity." Therefore, 1,656 years after the Creation (or 2,242 or 1,307 depending on the version of the Bible you consult), Earth was ruled by utter depravity, not just among the descendants of Cain but also among the more pious Sethites.

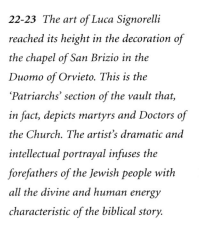

22-23 The art of Luca Signorelli reached its height in the decoration of the chapel of San Brizio in the Duomo of Orvieto. This is the 'Patriarchs' section of the vault that, in fact, depicts martyrs and Doctors of the Church. The artist's dramatic and intellectual portrayal infuses the forefathers of the Jewish people with all the divine and human energy characteristic of the biblical story.

23 In contrast, the hieratic figures in the Cupola della Scarsella in Florence's Baptistery radiate a sense of luminous, detached mysticism reinforced by the four figures in the center of the mosaic: the hierarchy here is superhuman.

Naamah invented spinning and weaving.

While the Cainites devoted themselves to mundane activities in the mysterious city of Enochia and surrounding region, their cousins descended from Seth (Adam and Eve's third son, "to console them for the loss of Abel") populated Mesopotamia and "invoked the name of the Lord." That is, they worshipped God while the others produced plows and looms. The worshippers lived long: Adam died at 930 years of age (Seth was conceived when Adam was 130), and of the nine patriarchs who were his direct descendants listed in the Bible, Enoch "walked with God" at a mere 365 years of age, whereas Methusaleh lived to be 969. But, as a devoted 19th-century Bible scholar, Father Fillion, explained, "if

In addition, the members of the two branches of the family had begun to intermarry. So God "saw that the wickedness of man was great in the earth" and regretted that he had created him, and decided to destroy him. (Adam had predicted this; in fact, he had prophesied twofold destruction, by fire and by the rising of high water. On this score, his descendants had taken pains to gain as much knowledge as possible, and had all that was known inscribed on two columns, one made of brick and the other of stone.)

One of the two, comments Flavius Josephus in his *Jewish Antiquities* (completed in 93/4 AD), was still standing in his time in the land of Siriada (a place which is not Syria and to which no other text refers).

The patriarch Noah

In those depraved times, there was only one "just and perfect man," the patriarch Noah. The Lord told him of his decision to destroy mankind, but said that Noah and his family would be saved so that the patriarch would be the head of a better race of human beings. God had the goodness to postpone the flood by 120 years so that Noah and his family could build the huge ark to escape the waters, together with "clean and unclean" beasts. When the vessel was ready (much more than a ship, it was a gigantic floating container), Noah received the order to load the animals and to enter it with his wife, their three sons and respective wives. The creatures of the Earth were taken aboard as follows: seven pairs each of all the "pure" animals, i.e., those it was permitted to eat, and one pair each of all the "impure" animals. There was a further delay of 7 days, then "the windows of heaven were opened." It rained for 40 days and nights uninterruptedly. All the land was submerged and it remained that way for another 150 days. In the end the water level began to drop until the ark, which drifted without any means of steering, came to rest "upon the mountains of Ararat" in Armenia. Noah sent out a raven — an unclean bird — which, having found food to eat in the floating bodies, did not return. Eight days later it was the turn of the dove, but it returned having found no place to rest its foot. Seven days later, Noah sent out the dove again, and this time it returned with an olive leaf in its beak. On the third occasion it was sent out, the dove did not return, having found land on which to rest, thus signaling that dry land had been found. Every form of life had been swept away because "fifteen cubits upward [roughly 25 feet] did the waters prevail; and the mountains were covered." The eight survivors waited for a formal divine order, then left the ark, and sacrificed a number of animals in thanksgiving. God appreciated the gesture and promised not to send another flood, and as a sign of his re-established alliance with man, he showed them a phenomenon they had never seen before, a rainbow.

26-27 *Genesis 6, 15 gives the size of the ark and specifies its decks ('… the length shall be 300 cubits, the breadth 50 cubits and the height 30 cubits … and with lower, second and third stories shalt thou make it') but not its layout. At the end of the 17th century, the Jesuit scholar Athanasius Kircher applied his scientific mind to this problem. He drew up this cross- section, with birds and quarters for humans on the upper deck, stores on the middle deck, and four-footed creatures on the lower deck.*

28 and 29 On the vault of the atrium in St. Mark's Basilica, Venice, a 13th-century cycle of Byzantine mosaics tells the story of Noah and the Flood. The first three episodes here show the loading of the ark. The various species are divided according to their ritual 'cleanliness,' following the dietary restrictions laid down in Leviticus, 11. Seven pairs of each clean animal were to be taken aboard, but only two pairs of each unclean animal, which included the pig and camel. Then the Flood is shown, with an evocative illustration of humanity perishing in the torrential rain, and the release and return of the dove. The crow, an impure bird, was first released by Noah, but, finding it could feast on the floating bodies (see detail, bottom left), it did not return. Beneath the rainbow that sealed the covenant with God, the ark is unloaded. Finally, the patriarch offers a dove on a sacrificial altar.

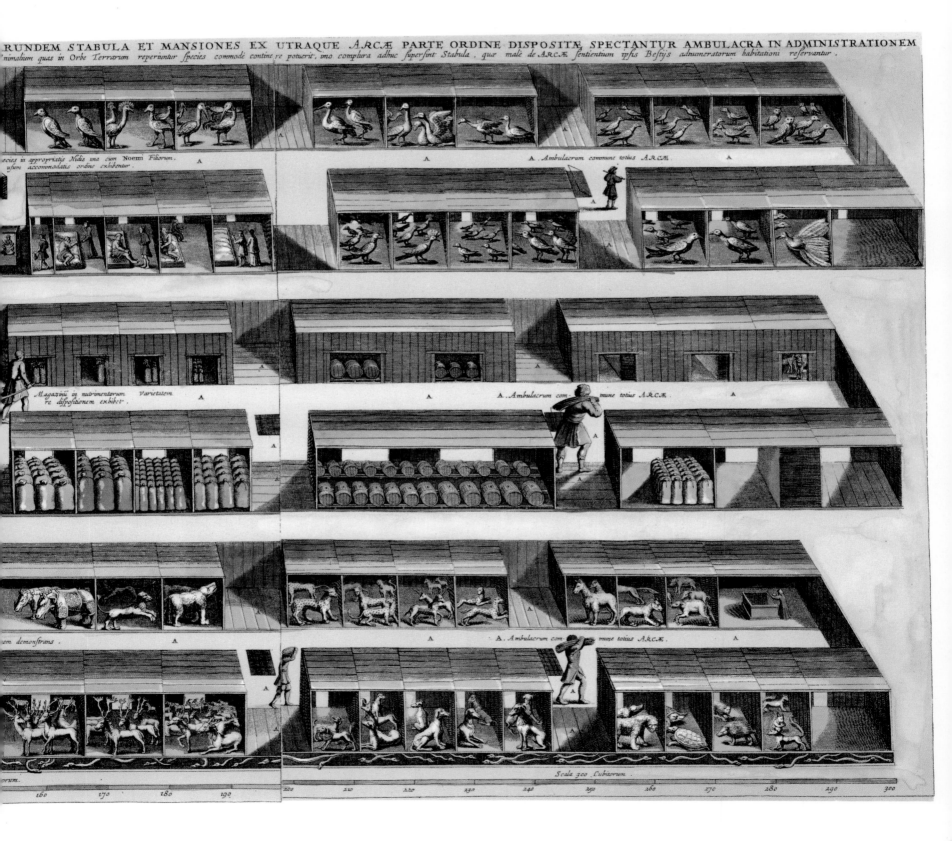

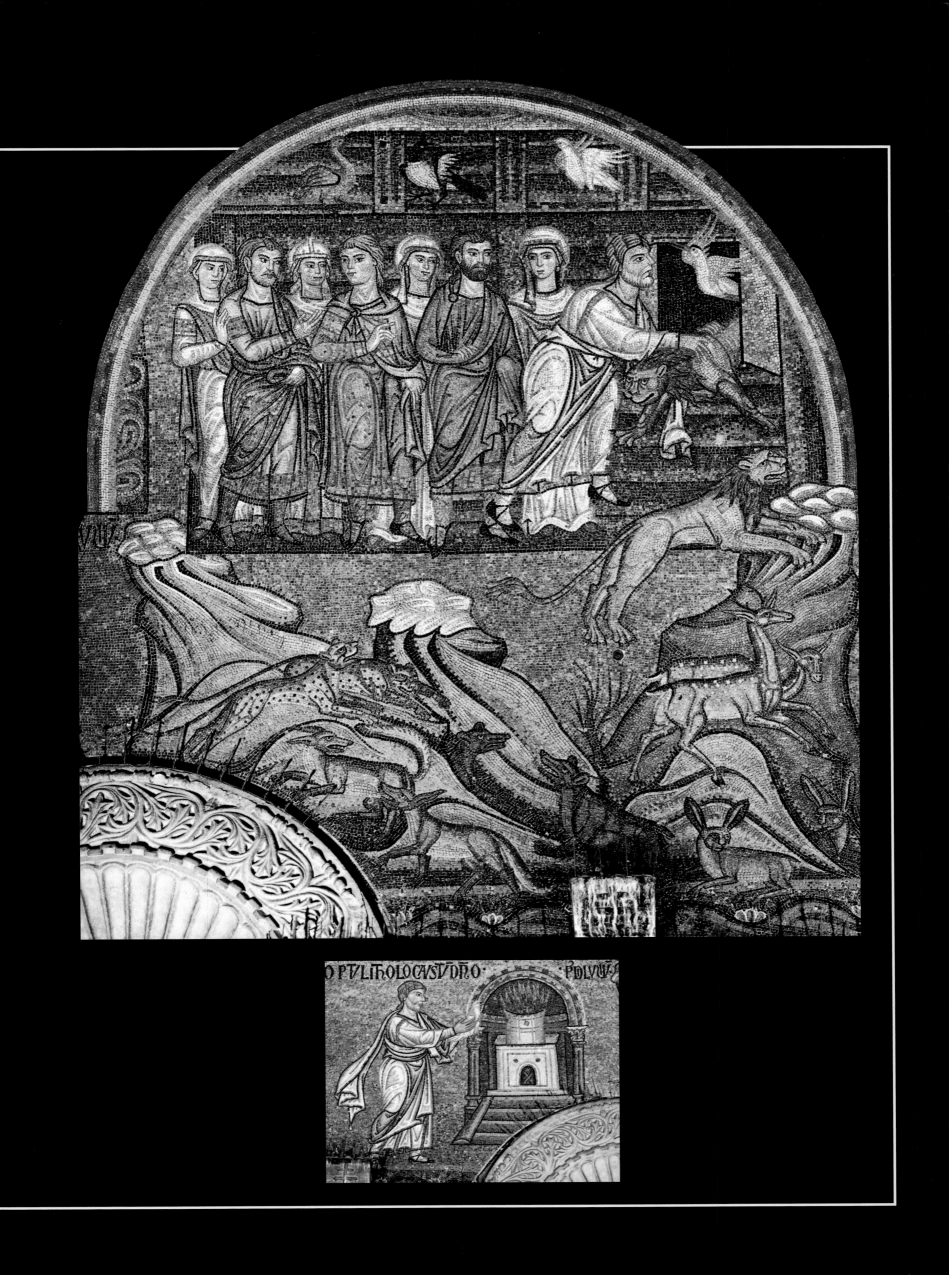

30 Representations of Noah's ark are varied and numerous, but have generally agreed on the positioning of the decks. In this series taken from 14th- and early 15th-century manuscripts, the shapes of the ark are unusual, although the images top right and center left – dated respectively 1411 and 1400-07 – are closer to the 'round boats' that date back much earlier, to Sumerian times.

31 Beneath a finally serene sky, after God had 'made a wind to pass over the earth,' the ark floated on a desert of water that, after forty days of uninterrupted rain, had risen 'fifteen cubits above the tops of the mountains.' The biblical account of the Flood seems to have a link with the Babylonian epic story of Gilgamesh in which the only man to survive the flood, Ut-napishtim, held the secret of immortality.

fac tibi archā de lignis leuigatis mēsiuculas i archa facies/et bitumine
linies, ex animātibz mūdis tolles septēna et septēna . ge. vi°. et vij°. c.

Omon dessus mētionnee
nous fut clerement fi
guree par les deux nom
bres septēnaires des bestes mūdes

32-33 *The clouds that shroud Mount Ararat continue to veil its mystery. The Bible cites the 'Ararat mountains' as the place where Noah's ark came to rest so clearly that travelers, scholars and philosophers have been interested in it for centuries. This interest has never waned, and 'sightings' and fruitless searches for pieces of wood on these treeless slopes continue.*

33 *Since the 19th century, Gustave Doré's illustration has been the most familiar image of the ark. He depicts like an enormous walnut shell with a superstructure like a palace, almost a temple. Dozens of dead bodies crowd his depiction, dominated at the center by the ark and by the dove that casts light into the darkness.*

Mount Ararat

As God had promised the ark would no longer be of use, it was abandoned on Ararat, and its remains still lie there according to some scholars. This tradition is very ancient. Josephus (writing at the end of the 1st century AD), said, "The Armenians call that place the place of the descent, and still in our time show the remains of the ark that was saved there." Three centuries earlier, Berosus, the Chaldean author of a *History of Babylon* of which nothing remains except a few fragments, recorded the custom of the mountain dwellers there of taking tiny particles of the bitumen that was used to caulk the hull, which they wore as a talisman against poisons. And the Greek philosopher Nicolaus of Damascus, who died shortly after the start of the Christian era, wrote in a *Universal History* that has since been lost: "Above Miniad in Armenia there is a large mountain called Baris [another name for Ararat], where it is said that many who survived the time of the flood were saved; and that a man in an ark berthed there on the peak and that the wooden remnants remained there for a long time."

They remained there still in the 4th century, at least according to St. John Chrysostom, the Patriarch of Constantinople, who used to mention them in his sermons as proof of the divine wrath that had punished the sinners. In the Middle Ages all travelers that passed that point, including Marco Polo, referred to Ararat as the place of the ark, adding however that no one was able to climb the mountain as the way was barred either by the perennial snows or by the will of God. During the Byzantine era, the Greek Orthodox Christians who lived in what is today Anatolia recounted the exploit of the monk James of Medzpin, who became Bishop of Nisibis (in northeast Mesopotamia) and was later canonized. Anxious to see the ark, he had long prayed to God to allow him that grace and finally began to climb the mountain. Tired and plagued by thirst, he stopped to rest, and, when he awoke, he saw a spring miraculously gushing before his eyes. ("James's Well" still exists and is one of the landmarks for modern searchers for the ark). Wending his way ever higher, every time the monk stopped for a short restful sleep, he awoke to find himself lower down the mountainside, at the same point from which he had started. He then understood that God did not want him to make the climb, and this was confirmed when an angel visited him to ask him to discontinue his attempt, and gave James a fragment of the ark saying that the sight of the ark was forbidden to man. This prohibition still seems to be in force as none of the expeditions that have explored Ararat since the early 19th century have found anything tangible.

THE TOWER OF ℬABEL AND THE SCATTERING OF THE PEOPLES

36 A series of blows led from the Original Sin to the 'corruption of the human race' and the destruction of humanity apart from Noah and his family. Not many generations passed before Earth witnessed a new insult to God. If not the most serious, the Tower of Babel was certainly the most striking. This illuminated drawing from the 15th-century Grimani Breviary shows the Tower during construction.

37 This illustration of the exodus from Noah's ark is taken from the Bedford Book of Hours (1423). Top, the animals disembark and wander off into the purified world; bottom right, the main episode in which Noah lies drunk and exposed after trying the juice of the vine. The next woes to befall humanity were to be caused by the mockery of Ham, Noah's third son.

PLATAVITVINEBIBESP:VNTIEBRIAGETNVDATABNATOSOPDCVVIDSSET
PATSVICENVDANTAVDVOB

+NOEP:EXIVTPARCEDEOLIO

+ATVEROSEMTIAFETPALIVTPOSVERTTMERISSVISTICEDENTESRETRO
FACESQEORAVSEERATAPATSVRILANOVDERTTVGILASATNOEEXVNOERDIOLS
AITMALEDETSCHANANSERVVSSERVOERTFRABSSIS:

Noah's descendants

oah had three sons, all of whom lived to be centenarians (Noah himself was 600 at the time of the Flood), but in those days, a centenarian was little more than an adolescent. The three sons were named Shem, Japheth and Ham; the first two were serious young men but Ham was rather careless, as was shown by his behavior when he found his father in lying drunk and "uncovered within his tent." Noah's drunkenness was the result of his discovery that the fruit of the vine (a plant that grew naturally in the region around Ararat) produced an inebriating drink called wine. The imprudent patriarch had drunk too much, perhaps unknowingly, and fallen into a deep sleep. Shem and Japheth covered their father respectfully with his cloak by walking backwards so as not to see his nakedness, but Ham inconsiderately laughed at his father. When he returned to consciousness, Noah learned of what had happened and placed a curse on his son that had effects for many generations. He decreed that Ham's descendants (usually referred to as Canaanites in the Bible) were to be the slaves of his two brothers and their descendants: these were the Semites (from Shem), who one day were to become a part of "God's people," and the Japhethites, who were to dominate a great part of the world and were to be converted to the God of the Jews. Bible commentators were later to interpret this divine three-way division of the Earth and its peoples as referring to Africans, the Jews, and Europeans.

One of the names in the long list of peoples and individuals descended from the three sons of Noah stands out. It is Nimrod, the grandson of Ham, who was "a mighty hunter before the Lord" and the founder of the first Babylonian empire in the vast land of Shinar that lay between the lower stretches of the Tigris and Euphrates. There Nimrod founded four cities: Babel (Babylon), Erech (Orchoë to the Greeks and now named Warka, which lies on the left bank of the Euphrates), Akkad, and Calneh (on the east bank of the Tigris where the city of Ctesiphon was to stand). Not content with all this, he went north and conquered Assyria from the Semites and founded four other cities. Of these Nineveh was to become the most famous, while of Resen, the "great city between Nineveh and Calah," nothing is known.

38-39 The mosaics of the stories of Noah and the Flood in the atrium in St. Mark's, Venice, illustrate the episodes that led the patriarch to place a curse on the descendants of Canaan (Genesis, 9, 18-29) after Ham (Canaan's father) had mocked him. The Canaanites were destined to be the servants of the lines descending from Shem and Japheth. In fact, the Canaanites, an indigenous people of Palestine, were overrun by the Israelites and, from the 18th century BC, lost control of all their cities and strongholds. The last scene shows the burial of Noah, who lived for a further 350 years after the Flood, dying at the age of 950.

The tower of pride

But Nimrod's ambitions were still not satisfied. He wanted to offer a challenge to God, and decided to build a tower "whose top may reach unto heaven," higher even than the waters of the flood had reached. Then, if the Lord wanted to inundate the Earth once more, the inhabitants could escape his wrath by climbing the tower.

There were no stones in the land of Shinar, so for months and months clay bricks were made, and baked in the sun or oven to line the outer walls so that the water would not enter. Day after day the tower grew higher, "higher than they had hoped" says Josephus, "its width was so great that in comparison its height seemed as nothing."

God came down to see what the army of men was building, and when he saw the size of the tower and that it would reach to heaven, he decided to bring a halt to their impiety. So he threw the descendants of Adam, who till that moment had all spoken one language, into confusion by giving them different languages. The work was brought to a halt by their inability to understand one another, however hard they tried, and the Lord "scattered them abroad across the face of the earth."

Today, thousands of years later, it seems that the divine curse fell fully on the proud city; archaeologists have shown that the remains of ancient Babylon were like a chaotic building site abandoned by its workers as soon as the lunch siren went.

40-41 In the vision of Pieter Bruegel the Elder (1525-1569), the Tower of Babel stands in the pleasant Flemish countryside, very different from Mesopotamia, where Nimrod, a descendant of Ham, decided to build a tower tall enough to challenge God. The biblical reference to the building materials – baked clay bricks – is significant, as the Mesopotamian civilizations used these in their construction of ziggurats (towers crowned by a temple).

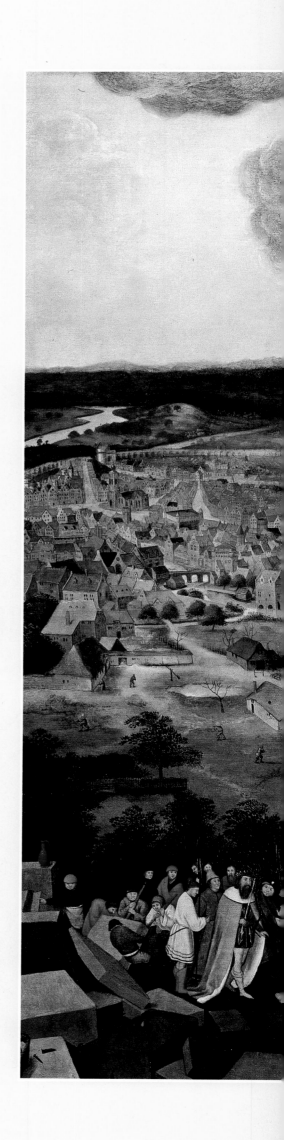

*42 God unleashed His anger on the Tower, throwing
Nimrod (in armor) and the Babylonians into
consternation. The picture is taken from the* Chronique
Universelle *of Jean de Courcy (circa 1470). God's
punishment of instilling the people with different languages
and scattering them across the world fascinated
Christendom, in particular after the actual linguistic
confusion and migrations that followed the downfall
of the Roman Empire.*

43 left *This illustration in a Latin breviary (1475-1500)
gives the Tower of Babel's construction a late medieval
setting typical of the 'age of the cathedrals.' Indeed, the
blocks of stone used are more typical of a Gothic church
than a Babylonian ziggurat.*

43 right *The depiction of the construction of the Tower of
Babel – taken here from a French codex, perhaps Parisian,
circa 1250 – allows the artists to show the tools and skills
of medieval Christendom: for example, the large man-
powered winches used to raise the stone, and the
transportation, shaping and use of the blocks.*

The forbidden tower – a myth created perhaps by the amazement of nomadic desert tribes who saw the ziggurats that rose above the walls of the Mesopotamian cities – has always fascinated man. In the 17th century, a learned Jesuit, Father Athanasius Kircher, who had already attempted to decipher Egyptian hieroglyphics and to work out the size of Noah's ark, wished to apply a scientific approach to the myth. Kircher calculated how many people could have populated the Earth over the period of 275 years from the Flood to the construction of the tower. Supposing that every Semite, Canaanite and Japhethite couple had had one child per year for a period of fourteen fertile years, a total of 9,094,468 men and women would have been born. He assigned half that total to the construction of the tower, i.e., 4,547,234, as the others would have been too young, too old or busy with other duties, for example, cultivating the land, looking after livestock or preparing food for the workers.

Kircher then examined "how high the tower would have to have been if they wished to reach the first heaven," that is, the heaven of Moon. On the basis of the astronomical knowledge of the time, he concluded it had to be 178,672 Italic miles high (an Italic mile used to equal approximately 1,620 yards), and, in order to support such a height, the base would have had to be 50 square Italic miles in size. After complicated operations, Kircher established that the number of bricks required was 374,354,625,000,000,000 – "a number so large that it is difficult to conceive."

Having completed all these calculations, he passed triumphantly to four conclusions.

First, if 4 million people had worked continuously for 3,426 years and the tower had risen by a mile a week, it would not have been completed even in that time.

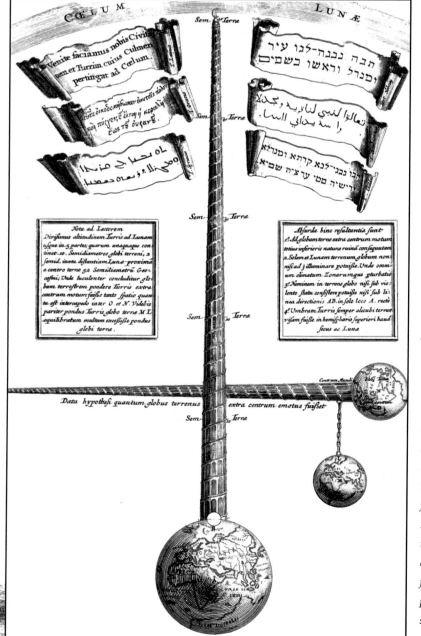

44 *The slender spire on the left is the Babylonian ziggurat as envisaged by the Jesuit scholar Athanasius Kircher who, at the end of the 17th century, applied a scientific viewpoint to the various problems posed by the Bible. The German clearly showed (right) the madness of building a tower that could reach the sky at its lowest point, that of the Moon, not to mention the Empyrean. In addition to other factors, the weight of the building would have pushed the Earth out of its position at the center of the Universe.*

45 *This late 17th-century engraving shows the cities built by Nimrod and his successors. Dominant in the center is Nineveh, founded by Ninus, the first king of Assyria. Nimrod's Babylon, with the Tower of Babel to the southeast, stands at the confluence of the Tigris and Euphrates, i.e., much further south than its historical position, although the city was situated where the two rivers came closest together.*

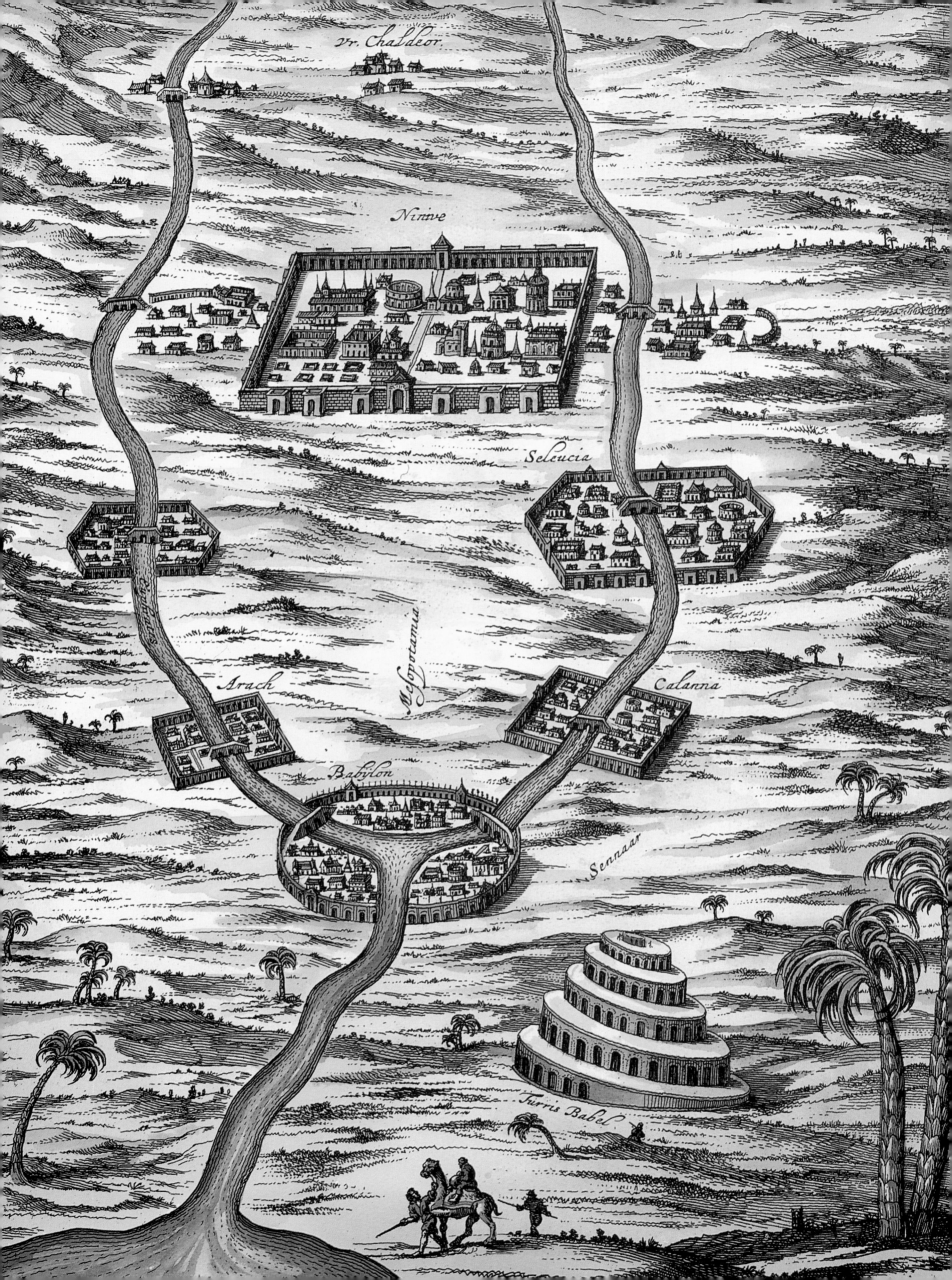

Vr. Chaldæor.

Ninive

Seleucia

Mesopotamia

Arach

Calanna

Babylon

Sennaar

Turris Babel

Second, if all the wood in all the forests of the world had been concentrated in that single place, and if the Earth had been made entirely of "lime and clay," and if the ocean with all the seas and rivers had been turned into bitumen, there would not have been enough wood to bake the bricks, nor clay to make the lime, nor ocean to make the bitumen.

Third, if a horseman had climbed the spiral slope for 30 miles a day, he would not have reached the top even after 800 years.

Fourth, the weight of the tower would have exceeded that of the Earth "by many parasangas" (an ancient Persian unit of measurement). "Let us suppose for a moment that the tower had been raised on Earth using materials supplied divinely. In this case, the Earth would have been pushed from the center of the universe by the excessive weight of the tower on top of the weight of the Earth … and if the globe had fallen, the entire world would have been ruined. Therefore, it was a vain and foolish presumption of man, I will not say to attempt, but even to think of such an enterprise; and deservedly God punished us with such a confusion of languages."

As with the discussions on the language Adam and Eve spoke in the Garden of Eden, the learned men of the past argued vociferously on the original language common to all men before God's punishment. Hebrew, naturally, was the most widely supported but there were plenty of other imaginative claims. The caustic Voltaire loved to tell the story of a lady at court in Versailles who often used to repeat: "Pity, without all that fuss over the Tower of Babel, today the whole world would speak French."

During the 17th century – an age devoted to scientific precision, as illustrated by Father Kircher – some German scholars, who supported Hebrew as the original language, proposed abandoning two newly born children in the forest. They were convinced that without human influence the two would spontaneously have spouted the original language of the Old Testament as soon as they were old enough to speak. They also pointed out subsidiary benefits to be had, such as knowing from the children's own mouths the correct pronunciation and syntax of the sacred idiom, whose purity had been lost over the course of the centuries, and thus rediscover "the language of the Holy Spirit."

46 and 47 The spiral structure of the 9th century minaret at Samarra (today in Iraq), about 60 miles northeast of Baghdad, immediately calls to mind certain illustrations of the Tower of Babel; e.g., the engravings of C. Decker on the page opposite (circa 1670). In fact, it is probable that this artist, like Bruegel and Kircher, was inspired by the information available on the earliest forms of Islamic minarets.

Hæc ruet eversis nunquam BABILONIA MURIS
Stans memori qua antum steterit Kircherius Orbi

Confusio linguarum

48 *The Tower of Babel at the height of its splendor – or, rather, pride – reaches the sky in this 17th-century Dutch school painting. Nimrod, visible in regal dress in the bottom left corner, watches his work, ignorant of the diaspora that will shortly follow.*

49 *In dramatic contrast, this work of the same period illustrates the result of human arrogance. Despite the emphasis placed on the disaster, Genesis, 11, 8-9 describes the episode without sensation: 'So the Lord scattered them abroad from thence upon the face of all the earth: and they left off to build the city. Therefore is the name of it called Babel' – from a word that meant 'confusion.' Over the centuries many theories were put forward on the language spoken before the advent of Babel, given the importance attributed to the language of Adam, i.e., the original and, therefore, the divine and perfect language.*

ABRAHAM, ESAU AND JACOB: JOSEPH IN EGYPT

50 The patriarch Abraham and his wife Sarah are seen in the center of a 17th-century Russian icon. The advent of the 'Father of many peoples' (the meaning of the name Abraham) marked a turning point in the Bible: having lost an earthly paradise, with Abraham we hear of the Land of Milk and Honey. This was clearly no Eden, but its name has long echoed down the centuries.

51 Inscribed in the capital letter A of the Souvigny Bible (a 12-century French manuscript), Abraham embraces the righteous. This association – linked to the Last Judgment – is characteristic of this patriarch and refers to the parable of the rich man in Luke 16, 19-31, in which Abraham welcomes the poor man and refuses the rich one with the words 'Remember that thou in thy lifetime receivedst good things.'

Abraham, the first of the patriarchs

Once the single people descended from Noah that had dared to climb to heaven had been scattered across the face of the world, it was divided into three races and myriads of lineages, hostile to one another and incapable of communication. The Bible abandons those sinners to their fate, and tells us no more of the universal story. Instead, it concentrates on a single family, the family of Abraham, which was destined for a great future.

Abraham, the son of Terah, was a direct descendant of Shem. He was born in Ur of the Chaldees around 2000 BC, a city of which little or nothing was known until eighty or so years ago. Even in the 19th century, people confused it with Urfa, which lay south of the Armenian mountains. It was, however, one of the largest cities in Mesopotamia, a metropolis of 250,000 people that lay on the right bank of the Euphrates between Babylon and the Persian Gulf. In Abraham's lifetime, Ur stood on a manmade mound surrounded by thick walls. Beginning in 1922, excavations led by Sir Leonard Woolley gradually brought ancient Ur to light, and with it a hitherto unknown civilization, that of the Sumerians.

The vast plain in which Ur stood was irrigated by a network of primary and secondary canals that carried water to the cereal fields, vegetable gardens and groves of date palms. All around there were farms and villages that supplied the large city with foodstuffs; Ur was a center that traded goods arriving down the Euphrates from the mountain region, and up the river from the sea.

The city was a labyrinth of narrow, twisting alleyways and passages no more than 7 feet wide that snaked between the buildings. The houses were made of clay, were cubic in shape, and had two floors and a flat roof. An internal courtyard, where many of the daily activities were performed, allowed light and air to enter the rooms. The courtyards were where the merchants stored their goods, weavers prepared their cloths, and craftsmen worked metal, wood and stone. Family life took place on the upper floors and, given the hot and often muggy climate, also often on the roof where families would sleep during the summer nights. Of the many gods that these hardworking but peaceful people worshipped, the most important was the Moon.

Ur was governed by a king and queen, and, when one of them died, courtiers, soldiers and musicians would dress in their best clothes, sit in an orderly manner around the corpse, and drink a cup of poison to accompany and serve the dead monarch in the Afterworld.

52 In the church of Santa Maria Novella, Florence, Filippino Lippi painted Abraham in anguish with his knife in his hand. The reference is to the sacrifice of his son Isaac, but the pain that the observer feels is also given by knowledge of the age in which the artist lived, at the waning of the greatness of 15th-century Florence.

53 Departing from Ur, his birthplace and the splendid capital of Sumeria, Abraham was obliged to pass by the sacred ziggurat whose ruins still remain on the Mesopotamian plain. The magnificent monument was built by King Ur-Nammu at the end of the 22nd century BC, roughly one hundred years before the lifetime of Abraham.

In the land of Haran

Terah lived in this rich and refined city where the arts, literature and music were celebrated. He was probably a merchant and owned a large house with ten or perhaps even twenty rooms. One day, we do not know why, Terah decided to gather together everything he had and to head off with his family northwest towards Haran, about 625 miles away. Haran was another trading center at a crossroads on the caravan routes that crossed the Padan-aram plain. It may have been a business trip, or perhaps Terah, from the line of Shem, was simply carrying out the inscrutable designs of God, for it was in that city that the Lord ordered Abraham (who at that time was a whippersnapper of 75) to leave. "Get thee out of thy country, and from thy kindred, and from thy father's house, unto a land that I will shew thee," said the Lord, promising that in exchange Abraham would be blessed and his name would resound down the ages.

54 top This 13th-century illuminated letter shows Abraham listening to the voice of the Lord. Here Abraham is the prototype of the true servant of God, the man who diligently follows instructions from on high, and who stoically obeys His orders: 'And he believed in the Lord and he counted it to Him for righteousness' (Genesis 15, 6). The indestructibility of Abraham's faith was a fundamental aspect of this complex figure; as the father of Ishmael – the forefather of the Arab tribes – he is also considered a prophet in the Islamic faith.

54 bottom and 54-55 The boundless grazing lands on Syria's borders are still used by herders living an 'archaic' life that follows changeless rhythms and patterns. On his first two journeys to Canaan, Abraham passed through this featureless plain, which lay between Mesopotamia and Assyria. In what is today Syria, the patriarch received from God the promise of a new land in which his descendants would be glorious and numerous.

Journey to Canaan

So Abraham left with his wife Sarah and his nephew Lot and all their belongings. They took the road toward Egypt that passes by the oasis of Tadmor, which the Romans later called Palmyra, and which did not yet have the magnificent pagan temples whose ruins can be seen today. He passed by Damascus, that claims to be the oldest uninterruptedly inhabited city in the world, and which stands to the northeast of the snow-capped Mount Hermon. Then he crossed the river Jordan and finally entered Canaan, which, at the time, belonged to the pharaoh of Egypt. This was his destination because the Lord appeared to him saying, "Unto thy seed will I give this land." But Abraham did not stop there because he was the chief of a tribe of herders and had with him hundreds of people, goats and cattle; they needed pastureland and knew that the Canaanites were always hostile to nomadic herdsmen. So, after building two altars to the Lord, he continued south toward Egypt because Canaan was suffering a drought and his livestock was at risk.

He entered Egypt distrustful of the libidinous customs of its people. His wife was very lovely and he was afraid that he might be killed by someone who wished to take her from him, so he asked Sarah to pretend to be his sister. This precaution was justified because, when the pharaoh saw Sarah, he took her to his palace but Sarah told the pharaoh she was Abraham's wife, whereupon he let her go. However, he let Abraham know that he was displeased at having been tricked and asked Abraham to leave the country.

The group crossed the sterile solitude of the Sinai and returned to Canaan but there was insufficient grazing for the entire family's animals, so Abraham decided to separate from his nephew Lot. Abraham would take his family and goods up into the hills, while Lot would stay with his goods and animals in the plain near a city called Sodom. However, Abraham and his men were soon obliged to come down from the hills to fight the armies of "four kings" who had come down from the north and taken Lot and his family prisoner. They freed their relations and received the congratulations of the king of Sodom for having chased away the invaders from the north. Abraham and his tribe prospered but, despite God's promises to give Abraham an heir, Sarah remained barren. So Sarah advised her husband to take Hagar, her Egyptian maid, as his wife and bear children by her. And Hagar gave birth to Ishmael, who was destined to be the forefather of the Arab people.

When Ishmael was born, Abraham was 86 but he had to wait until he was 99 before the Lord came to him to announce that finally he would have a son by Sarah and that he was to be called Isaac. The boy was to be circumcised so that his descendants would be distinguished from other peoples.

Shortly afterward, God appeared once more to Abraham as he was sitting before his tent 'in the heat of the day' in the plains of Mamre. He came in the form of a man and had with him two angels who were also in the form of men. This meeting took place close to Hebron and is traditionally identified by a grove of thorn bushes close to a terebinth tree (which is said to have grown from the staff planted in the ground by the angels). The Roman emperor Constantine built a basilica here and the Arabs call the place Mamet el-Khalil.

56-57 and 56 bottom In the luminous mosaics in St. Mark's Basilica, Venice, Abraham is shown with his wife Sarah, his nephew Lot and the servants 'acquired in Haran' on their way to Canaan, the land that God will soon promise him.

57 In Les Petites Heures *commissioned by Jean, duke of Berry (1340-1416), Abraham welcomes God and the angels who have come to tell him that he will finally have a son by Sarah, and the boy is to be called Isaac.*

The flight from Sodom

The three visitors told Abraham that he would finally have his longed-for son by Sarah, though both of them were old. They stated that the cities in the plain – Sodom, Gomorrah, and another three that constituted the Pentapolis – would be destroyed by God's ire because they were filled with hardened sinners. And so it happened, though God had promised Abraham that he would spare them if he found just 10 good men there; but they were all iniquitous and the patriarch watched as a rain of brimstone and fire was sent down upon the cities and destroyed all forms of life. Shortly before, two angels had led the reluctant Lot, his wife and two daughters out of Sodom and given them the strict instruction not to look back at the city. Lot's wife could not resist, however, and was turned in an instant into a pillar of salt.

The terrorized Lot fled up onto a mountain and sheltered in a cave. His two daughters, despairing that no man would ever come up to them on the mountain and desperate to have children, got Lot drunk and each lay with him.

58-59 The iniquitous city of Sodom expiates its sins in the fire. This fresco of the school of Raphael adorns the Vatican Loggias and shows Lot (Abraham's nephew) and his two daughters fleeing to safety. His wife dares to look back despite God's instructions and, in consequence, is turned into a pillar of salt.

59 This painting of Sodom in flames is by Jan Bruegel (nicknamed 'Velvet Bruegel'). It demonstrates the Italian influence on the work, and, most suitably, blends the catastrophic visions of his father Pieter Bruegel the Elder and his brother Pieter Bruegel the Younger, also known as 'Hell Bruegel.'

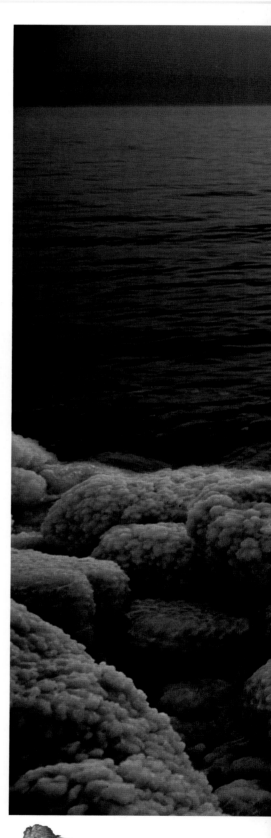

The Dead Sea

The two boys that resulted from these incestuous relationships were called Moab and Ammon, who became the forefathers of the Moabite and Ammonite people who settled east of the Jordan and the Dead Sea, and against whom the descendants of Abraham were to battle long and hard. Where were the five cities of the Pentapolis? At the time of Josephus (who said he had personally seen the pillar of salt of the curious wife), it was thought they lay at the southern tip of the Dead Sea where saline concentrations covered a series of strange forms that resembled buildings and petrified human beings. The book of Genesis suggests that the "five cities of the plain" were Sodom, Gomorrah, Admakh, Zeboim, and Bela. Moreover, a mountain in that same area is known to the Arabs as Gebel Usdun or Gebel Sudun. During the Middle Ages, Christian pilgrims used to visit that geological burial ground devoutly, but when St. Egeria passed that way in the 4th century, she said that the pillar was no longer there, adding, perhaps with a touch of malice, that it had been seen shortly before her arrival.

60 and 61 Salt, which is predominant in the Dead Sea and along its coastline, is naturally associated with sterility. The bizarre and evocative shapes of saline formations along Israel and Jordan's Dead Sea coasts (particularly between Israel's En Gedi and the Sedom potash deposits) are therefore naturally linked to the remains of the impious Pentapolis that included Sodom and Gomorrah. Here God 'overthrew … that which grew upon the ground' (Genesis 19, 25). Scholars like Josephus and many travelers during the Roman era and Middle Ages actually saw the pillar of salt that was Lot's unnamed wife.

The birth of Isaac

62 top *The sentimental and realistic painting style of Giovanni Francesco Barbieri (known as Guercino) perfectly suits the theme of Abraham's banishment of his wife Sarah's Egyptian slave and her son, Ishmael, who is seen here in tears next to his mother. The instigator of the unfair exile, caused by Ishmael's jealousy of Isaac, was Sarah, not Abraham, who was made unhappy by the event.*

62-63 *Veronese's portrayal of divine aid being provided to Hagar and her son Ishmael was set in a wood rather than in the Pharan desert, a desert of uncertain location but that may have been not far from the destroyed Pentapolis, i.e., southwest of the Dead Sea. Previously God had promised Hagar that her son would be the forefather of a line that would be too numerous to count (the Arab tribes), but had added that this line would never live in peace.*

A year after the destruction of Sodom and Gomorrah, the 90-year-old Sarah gave birth to Isaac, called "the son of laughter" because his father laughed with happiness when he saw him. Isaac's half-brother Ishmael was jealous of Isaac and, at Sarah's request, Abraham sent him away with Hagar, his mother. The exiles wandered in the wilderness of Beersheba. They risked death from hunger and thirst but God intervened and saved them by making a well appear before them.

Increasingly rich and powerful, Abraham allied himself to the king of the Philistines, Abimelech, from which he was given a well-watered region of Beersheba. He was happy as he finally had a legitimate heir but God requested that Abraham sacrifice his son as an offering. Racked with anguish but obedient, the old patriarch left with his son for Mount Moriah where the dreadful act was to be executed.

The Jews identify Mount Moriah, which is three days' walk from Beersheba, with the hill in Jerusalem on which Solomon's temple was later built. During the Middle Ages the place of the sacrifice was indicated as the rock that overlooks the dome of Omar's Mosque (the Dome of the Rock). This is the spot in which Abraham stood the stake on which he was to burn his son after having sacrificed him. He raised the knife over his son's body but was stopped by the voice of an angel, telling him that God had only wished to test Abraham's faith. From Beersheba, Abraham moved back to Hebron with his tribe where his wife Sarah died, at the age of 127. To bury her, Abraham bought a field that had a cave at one end near Mamre in a place named Machpelah. This became the family tomb where Abraham himself, Isaac and Rebecca, Leah and Jacob were later to be buried.

64 This 17th-century, gloomy Sacrifice of Isaac is
attributed to Salvator Rosa. Only a tenuous divine light
stops Abraham's knife at the supreme moment, and fixes the
moral significance of the story forever.

65 Sacred to the three great monotheistic religions, the rock
on which Abraham prepared to sacrifice his son has been
dominated since the 8th century by the dazzling Dome on the
Rock (Omar's Mosque), one of the holiest buildings in Islam.

After the Muslim conquest of the region (634-640), a mosque was built over the sacred spot, but after the First Crusade, during the short duration of the Crusaders' Kingdom of Jerusalem (1099-1187), a basilica replaced the mosque and Christian pilgrims to the Holy Land were able to enter the crypt. With the loss of the region again to the Muslims, a new mosque (the current one) was built on the ruins of the basilica. A 15th-century manuscript gives a report of a find (or invention, as it was called in those days) made on 25 June 1119 by the canons of the Latin priorate established in Hebron. They had discovered a well beneath their chapel, into which a monk named Arnulf descended that same day. He found two grottoes there: in one there were two skeletons, in the other he found fifteen vases filled with bones. Without further ado, the two skeletons were declared as belonging to Abraham and Isaac (who was buried at the feet of his father), and the bones in the vases as belonging to Jacob. Celebrations were held in the priorate for days on end. No mention is made of the women in the family. The Jews – and after them the Muslims – also claim this sacred place to be the tomb of Adam. During the credulous Middle Ages, custodians showed pilgrims from the three monotheistic religions the field of red earth that lay all around; this was where God was supposed to have made the first man. The custodians also showed the grotto in which Adam and Eve hid after being chased out of Eden, and even the field in which Cain killed Abel.

66 top Built as a church during the Crusades, Ibrahim's Mosque in Hebron is evidence of the alternating powers and faiths that have characterized the history of this city. According to the Bible, Sarah and then Abraham were buried in the cave of Machpelah in Kiriat Arbat (Hebron). When human remains were discovered in two caves beneath a chapel in Hebron, they were immediately attributed to the patriarch and his descendants, though without mention of Sarah.

66 bottom A narrow window beneath a shrine in Ibrahim's Mosque looks into Abraham's venerated burial chamber.

67 The cave of Machpelah is closed off by a silver gate and heavy silver lock. The furnishings of the crypt are entirely Islamic: Muslims worship Abraham (or rather Ibrahim, the father of Ismail) as one of the great prophets of their religion.

68 Baroque architecture typical of Bernini is sited in
the 'Roman' landscape in which Antoine Coypel set the
meeting between Abraham's servant and Isaac's future
bride. The patriarch sent his faithful servant to Haran –
where Abraham's relations still lived – to search for a
woman worthy to be his son's wife. He insisted on two
things: the woman was not one of the detested
Canaanites, and the choice of woman would not require
Abraham to take Isaac back to the land that God had
ordered Abraham to leave.

69 top The Neapolitan painter Andrea Vaccaro infused
a clearly defined light, in the style of Caravaggio, into
his mid 18th-century classical composition of the
Meeting between Rebecca and Isaac.

69 bottom Now blind, Isaac as an old man is deceived
by his wife Rebecca and blesses Jacob instead of Esau.
Painted in 1637 by Jusepe de Ribera, this masterpiece of
expressiveness is imbued with a particular clarity of
light.

Abraham's children

When Abraham felt close to the end of his life, he wanted to ensure his son Isaac was married suitably. He did not want him to marry an idolatrous Canaanite, so he sent a trusted servant to the distant plain of Haran, where his relations still lived. When close to the city of Nahor, the servant came across a lovely girl named Rebecca, who was descended from Abraham's line, as she drew water from the well. He took the girl back to Hebron where Rebecca married Isaac and gave birth to twins, Esau and Jacob. Jacob envied his brother, who was the first born, as this made him the heir to the family goods.

Taking advantage of Esau's exhaustion one day when he returned from working in the fields, Jacob persuaded his brother to sell his birthright in exchange for a plate of lentils, but later Esau regretted his action and threatened to kill Jacob. His mother Rebecca saved Jacob by sending him to the house of her brother Laban in Haran.

Jacob in Haran

During his journey there, Jacob dreamed of a ladder that reached up to the sky and heard the voice of the Lord telling him that he would inherit the land of Canaan.

Once he arrived in Haran, Jacob earned his living as a watchman of his uncle's herds during which time he fell in love with Laban's younger daughter, the beautiful Rachel. Laban agreed that the two should marry as long as Jacob worked for him for seven years, but when the period was finally over, Laban tricked Jacob by making him marry the elder daughter Leah, who, according to custom, wore a veil at the ceremony. Jacob did not give in, and agreed to work for a further seven years to earn himself Rachel. After their marriage, he left Haran with his two wives and animals to return to Canaan to find that, in the meantime, his brother Esau had married a Canaanite and thus disengaged himself from the Chosen People. This couple became the progenitors of the Edomite line, against which the Jews were later to fight.

On his way back to Canaan Jacob had to cross the River Jabbok. He was briefly left alone on the right bank after having ensured his family, animals and servants had crossed first. He found he was obliged to wrestle an unknown man, whom he fought until daybreak but, neither of the two getting the upper hand, the stranger touched the hollow of Jacob's thigh and put it out of joint. Jacob understood that this stranger was an angel of the Lord and asked to be blessed. The angel told Jacob that he was no longer to be called Jacob but Israel, meaning "he who fights with God."

70 *The theme of divine promise was presented once more in a visionary manner in Jacob's dream, in which Jacob was promised the land of Canaan and numerous offspring. Depicted here in a 16th-century work of the Avignon school, Isaac's son rests his head on the stone that, according to the oath he was to make when he awoke, would be 'the house of God.'*

71 *Dizzying yet diaphanous, Jacob's ladder, painted here by Luca Giordano, heralds the new pictorial language of the 18th century. Light is no longer bound to naturalistic realism, and, very suitable in this scene, is more celestial than terrestrial.*

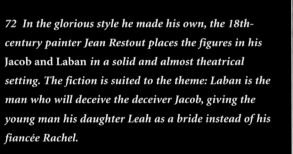

72 In the glorious style he made his own, the 18th-century painter Jean Restout places the figures in his Jacob and Laban *in a solid and almost theatrical setting. The fiction is suited to the theme: Laban is the man who will deceive the deceiver Jacob, giving the young man his daughter Leah as a bride instead of his fiancée Rachel.*

73 top Jacob 'rolled the stone from the well's mouth' to let Rachel's flock drink. This was the first meeting between Jacob and the young girl, whom he succeeded in marrying only after waiting fourteen years.

73 center Riding the bizarre camels painted in the Vatican Loggias by Raphael's pupils, Rachel and Leah flee with Jacob, his ten sons and all the flocks that Jacob had earned – more or less honestly – working for his uncle.

73 bottom The final phase in the flight of Jacob and his family is depicted here by the 18th-century painter Andrea di Leone. The family crosses the river Jabbok to reach their ancestral lands in Canaan.

74 *Jacob wrestles with the angel in a work by Eugene Delacroix (1850). This is crucial moment in the history of Israel: after the struggle, the angel tells Isaac's son, 'Thy name shall be … Israel, for as a prince hast thou power with God, and hast prevailed' (Genesis 32, 28).*

75 top *Vibrant colors and emotional intensity charge the atmosphere of Francesco Hayez' 1844 painting of the meeting between Jacob and Esau. The two brothers are reconciled but Esau's line will become the Edomites, who will be the future adversaries of the Jews.*

75 bottom *Restored during the Crusader era and then enclosed inside a Greek Orthodox monastery, the ancient Jacob's Well was dug by Isaac's son at Shechem, near Nablus, after his return from Mesopotamia.*

76-77 top *The dramatic events in the life of Joseph, Jacob's favorite son by his beloved wife Rachel, form the scenes in the superb 14th- and 15th-century Byzantine mosaics in the dome of the Baptistery in Florence. Jealousy and deceit are the themes in the story of the charming young man: first, he was betrayed by his many brothers, who also deceived Jacob by showing him Joseph's bloodstained coat and telling him that Joseph was dead. Then the brothers sold the young man to a caravan of traders who took him to Egypt and sold him there into slavery.*

76-77 bottom *Misfortune was followed by further misfortune. Granted intelligence and extreme ability by the Lord, but given the jealousy that these qualities arouse, Joseph earned the trust of his Egyptian master, Potiphar; however, the young man met further downfall when he was betrayed by Potiphar's wife. Having refused her advances, the woman accused him of attempting to seduce her and had him thrown into prison. Even in this dismal situation, Joseph succeeded in gaining the prison governor's trust.*

Joseph in Egypt

For more than thirty years Jacob's family and their herds lived in the land of Canaan. By Leah Jacob had 10 sons and by Rachel he had Joseph, but Joseph was his favorite. The ten half-brothers were jealous and hated Joseph so much that one day, when he was 17, they decided to kill him. Jacob, who was by now an old man, remained working in the fields while his sons took the animals to graze. Joseph was sent by his father to see how his brothers were doing, whom he found at the wells of Dothan near Bethulia. When they saw him arriving, they decided to put their plan into action but one of them, Reuben, wanted to save Joseph. He advised them not to spill the boy's blood but to throw him into a pit where he would die alone (in fact, it was Reuben's plan to return and to help Joseph out of the pit). They agreed, and when Joseph arrived, they stripped him of his coat of many colors given him by his father, and prepared to throw him into the pit. Before they could, however, they saw a caravan of Ishmaelites heading toward Egypt. One of the brothers,

named Judah, had the idea of selling the boy as a slave to the merchants. After doing this, they spilled ram's blood on Joseph's coat and took it back to their father, whom they convinced that Joseph had been eaten by a wild beast. At the time that Joseph was taken into Egypt by his Ishmaelite owners, the country was ruled by the people that Josephus calls the "Shepherd Kings" and whom we know as the Hyksos. They were a Semitic people from the east who had conquered the valley of the Nile and established their capital in Memphis (c. 1720 BC). Perhaps it was here that Joseph was sold as he was bought by one of the pharaoh's high functionaries named Potiphar, who was the commander of the palace guard. Being an intelligent boy, Joseph was soon made superintendent of the household by his master and put in charge of all things. As he was also young and good-looking, Potiphar's wife was attracted by the boy and several times bade him come to her bed but Joseph repeatedly refused. Offended, she accused him of attempted rape and Joseph was put in prison.

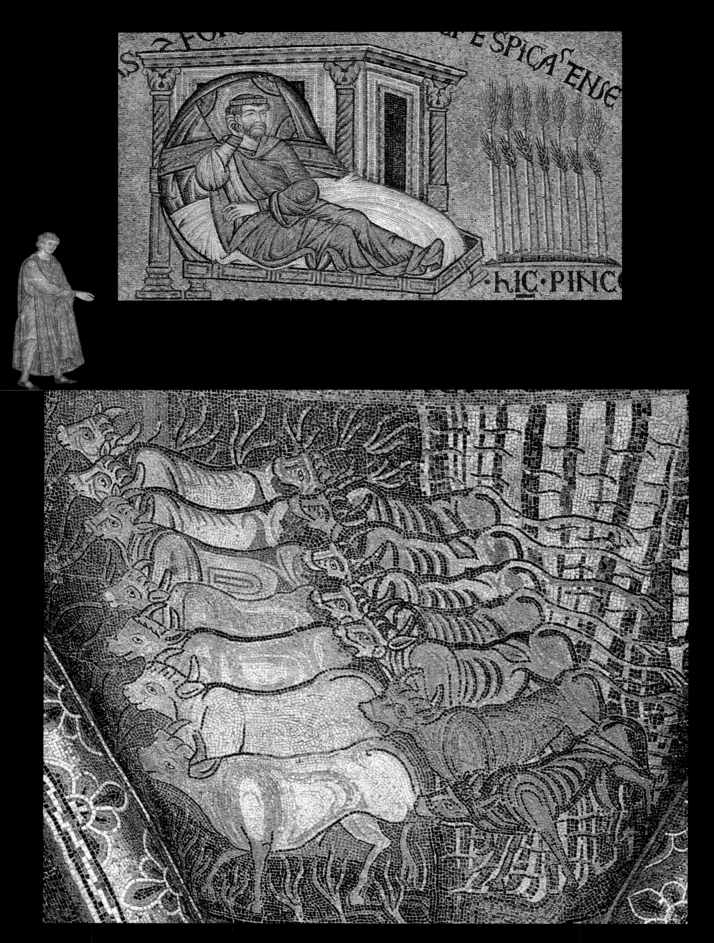

78 top *The pharaoh – shown here in a 13th-century mosaic in St. Mark's Basilica, Venice – dreams of seven ears of corn that are 'devoured' by seven thin ears (Genesis 41, 7).*

78 bottom *In another section of the mosaic, seven fat cows are devoured by seven 'ill-favored and lean' cattle (Genesis 41, 3). Having demonstrated his ability to interpret dreams in prison, Joseph was called to interpret the king's*

nightmares and concluded that the Lord wanted to announce the arrival of seven years of abundance followed by seven years of famine.

79 top *Joseph explains the meaning of the dreams to the pharaoh. Perhaps this ruler was a Hyksos, one of the 'shepherd kings' who governed Lower Egypt in the 17th and 16th centuries BC.*

The pharaoh's dreams

One of his gifts, however, was his ability to interpret dreams, thanks to which he predicted the future of several of his jail mates. One of them, a royal functionary before being imprisoned and then freed (as Joseph had predicted), spoke of Joseph to the pharaoh. After two years, the pharaoh had two dreams that no one was able to interpret, in which seven fat cows were eaten by seven thin cows, and seven heavy ears of corn were eaten by seven thin ears of corn.

79 center Revealing his ability to see the future, Joseph stores great quantities of crops to see Egypt through the years of famine (left) and distributes them at the right time (right). In this 13th-century mosaic in St. Mark's, note the pyramidal form of the 'granaries' used for storage purposes, an unusual reference to the Egyptian pyramids.

79 bottom Two imprisoned dignitaries of the pharaoh dream of their fate, which Joseph explains to them. The man on the left, the head cup-bearer in the pharaoh's court, dreams of three vines and a cup of wine to offer the pharaoh. The interpretation is that he will be freed from prison in three days. The man on the right, the head baker, dreams of three baskets of bread and a crow that eats the contents: he, on the other hand, will be hanged in three days.

Onfitcor tibi domine
em toto corde meo: quo
niam audicti uerba
oris mei. In con
fpetu angelorum pfal
lam tibi adorabo ad templum fanctum tu
um + confitebor nomini tuo. Sup mia
tua + ueritate tua: quoniam magnificacti
fup omne nomen fanctum tuum. In

Called to court, Joseph revealed the mystery of the dream: there would be seven years of abundance followed by seven years of famine, and, in order to live through the famine, large stores of grain needed to be laid by.

Impressed, the pharaoh took the ring from his finger and slipped it onto the finger of the Jewish slave. He had him dressed in fine linen, hung a gold chain around his neck and placed him on the first chariot after his own. When Joseph passed in public, the people were made to kneel in front of him.

Joseph was made the first minister of Egypt and given the daughter of the high priest of Heliopolis as a wife. The seven years of abundance gave way to the seven years of famine but because of Joseph's prediction Egypt did not suffer.

Canaan, on the other hand, was made desolate by the drought and Jacob decided to send his ten sons to the Nile valley as he had heard that corn was being sold there. He kept with him the youngest son, Benjamin, who was Joseph's younger brother by Rachel.

When the caravan arrived in Memphis, the first minister himself welcomed it, but none of the brothers recognized Joseph. After subjecting the brothers to a number of tests, Joseph made himself known to them during a second trip to Egypt in which Benjamin was included. With the agreement of the pharaoh, the entire family was invited to Egypt where they prospered.

At the age of 147, the patriarch Jacob died in Egypt, after having brought all his 12 sons together and predicted the future of his descendants, saying that they would be the forefathers of the 12 tribes of Israel. His body was embalmed in the Egyptian manner and taken to the cave of Machpelah accompanied by a large procession. After returning to Memphis with his brothers, Joseph lived for another 54 years "blessed by God and all men."

He died there but his final wish was that his bones be taken to the Promised Land when the people of Israel returned to settle there, in accordance with the wishes of God.

80 This illuminated page is taken from the Salisbury Psalter (prior to the Reformation, 1370-80). It shows the dying Jacob, called 'Israel' in Genesis 48, blessing the sons of Joseph. In reference to the episode in which the patriarch's epic history originated, the dream of the ladder is shown at the center of the initial letter. This event portended how God had promised Jacob a vast and glorious line of descendants.

81 top In a 14th-century mosaic in the Baptistery in Florence, Joseph, the viceroy of Egypt, reveals himself to his brothers, those who had sold him into slavery. He pardons them as everything that occurred was decided by a higher power: 'And God sent me before you to preserve you a posterity in the earth … So now it was not you that sent me hither but God' (Genesis 45, 7-8).

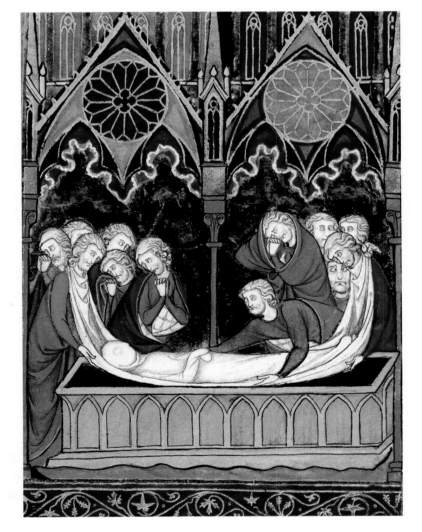

81 bottom Jacob's body has been mummified and placed in a sarcophagus, as was customary in Egypt, and is buried in Canaan as the 147-year-old patriarch requested. This illustration is taken from the San Luigi Psalter (1253-70). As Genesis 50 describes, when the body had been prepared, his relations and all the Egyptians mourned him for seventy days.

MOSES AND THE EXODUS

82 *In* Moses and the Ten Commandments *(circa 1620),
Guido Reni has captured all the authority and dramatic power
of the leader of the Jews. Moses led the Jews in the exodus
from Egypt and was the link between God and his Chosen
People. The tablets he holds are the sign of divine appointment,
whereas the reverential fearfulness on his face admirably
expresses his emotions following his meeting with God.*

83 *Moses' life is almost at an end, and with it the
wanderings of the Israelites after leaving Egypt. At the
top of Mount Nebo, an angel shows the old prophet the
Promised Land. In this detail of the* Testament and
Death of Moses *(Sistine Chapel, 1482) Luca Signorelli
instills the face of God's messenger with infinite
gentleness.*

Slavery in Egypt

For four doleful centuries, according to biblical chronology, the Jews remained in Egypt. The Egyptians, who, in the meantime, chased out the Hyksos and placed a new Egyptian dynasty on the throne (c. 1570 BC), transformed the Jews into slaves. According to Josephus, the Jews were forced to dig canals, build walls, embankments, cities and the pyramids, although of course the Egyptian pyramids had already existed for about 2,000 years. Josephus continues to say that all this occurred as a result of envy, because the Jews were hard workers who grew in number and were prosperous. What is more probable is that during the Egyptian struggle against the Hyksos, the Jews aligned themselves with the wrong side and that their slavery was the price they had to pay when the foreign pharaohs were defeated. This is

what is suggested by the story of Joseph, who was favored and protected by the pharaoh.

At the time of the Jews' migration from impoverished Canaan to the fertile Nile delta, the tribe led by Jacob-Israel, which was to divide into 12 branches, numbered about 70 people. Divine blessing meant they proliferated extraordinarily and, four hundred years later, there were hundreds of thousands of Jews in the province of Gessen, which lies between the cities of Heliopolis to the south, Bubastis to the west, and Tanis and Mendes to the north. They enjoyed a sort of independence under the administration of their 12 "princes," cultivating their lands and grazing their animals. Some had even become skilled craftsmen.

Unlike other immigrants that had been assimilated into the Egyptian population, the Jews had main-

84 top This attractive drawing by the French Egyptologist Émile Prisse d'Avennes, copied from a scene in Ramesses II's funerary temple, the Ramesseum, shows the pharaoh on his war chariot creating havoc among the Hittites. The intolerance toward foreigners that increased during his reign caused the Jews to leave Egypt and return to Canaan.

84-85 In the necropolis of Beni Hasan, the tomb of Khnumhotep – governor during the XII Dynasty – contains an illustration of the arrival in Egypt of a caravan of Semitic nomads. This reproduction is taken from The Monuments of Egypt and Nubia *(Vol. IV, plates XXVII and XXVIII) made by Ippolito Rosellini during the Franco-Tuscan archaeological expedition of 1828-29.*

tained their beliefs, customs, language and religion: they were, after all, the Chosen People. Perhaps this was why they were persecuted by Ramesses II around 1300 BC; the Jews, who were already allied with foreign conquerors, formed an extraneous community settled in a key region too close to Egypt's western border and to the fortifications of the Princes' Wall. The wall ran from the shore of the Mediterranean to Lake Timsah and prevented access to the country from the Sur desert to the northeast. This was the direction from which the Hittites – against whom the pharaoh was at war – would attack. Ramesses feared revolts and betrayal by those citizens of Egypt that had retained their own identity but also recognized them as a resource to transform the city of Tanis into his new capital (to be

named after himself) and to build a new city called Pithom slightly to the south.

So it was that the Jews were obliged to make the clay bricks and lay them under the eyes of supervisors, and the more that died, thought the pharaoh, the better it will be. But though they were exhausted by the work and maltreatment, the tough Jews did not die in great enough numbers; on the contrary, "the more they were oppressed, the greater their numbers grew." Ramesses resorted to more drastic measures and ordered the Jewish midwives to kill all male babies, but his orders were not obeyed as the midwives claimed that Jewish women were very strong and had no need of midwives to give birth. So Ramesses then called on his own people to throw newborn Jewish males into the rivers.

The birth of Moses

86 *Placed in a papyrus basket on the Nile by his mother to save him from the pharaoh's decree, Moses was found by the daughter of the king in a reed bed, perhaps similar to this marshy section of Lake Manzala, the largest body of water in the Nile delta.*

87 *The 16th-century fresco in the Vatican Loggias by painters of Raphael's circle shows the moment in the finding of the baby Moses in which the Egyptian princess pulls back the covers in the papyrus basket to reveal a Jewish boy.*

Many mothers attempted to save their children and one commentator wrote that the slaughter must have been a complete failure as, 80 years later, when they left Egypt, there were 2 million Jews and certainly they were not all old. At least one baby survived because God had great plans for him. He was the son of Amram and Jochabed, both of who were members of the tribe of Levi, and the brother of Miriam and Aaron. The mother succeeded in hiding him for three months after his birth but in the end she gave in and abandoned him in an "ark of bulrushes"' and placed him on the Nile.

The baby was named Moses ("saved from the waters") by the Egyptian girl who, when she went to bathe, found the chest in a reed bed. She was not just any Egyptian girl, but a princess, one of the pharaoh's daughters. She saw that the child was Jewish and knew that her father's orders were that the baby should die, but she was compassionate and accepted the proposal by the baby's sister – who had been watching from the bank – that she find a Jewish wet

nurse to feed the baby. Of course, the wet nurse was the child's mother but the princess either did not realize this or chose to ignore it.

As Moses grew, his mother brought him up to learn "the wisdom of the Egyptians" as St. Stephen was to say, quoting the Jewish tradition. The Bible does not speak about Moses' childhood but Josephus reports that one day the princess took Moses to court to present him to the pharaoh and asked that he should be made heir to the throne if she should not have sons. The pharaoh agreed, hugged the little boy and, as a sign of goodwill, placed the royal diadem on the boy's head. Moses, however, thought the royal insignia was a toy and rolled it on the ground and stamped on it. The high priest considered this an evil omen and implored the pharaoh to kill the child, as he would be the ruin of Egypt. Yet, perhaps for love of his daughter, or because he did not believe in the prophecy, the king not only saved Moses but adopted him and welcomed as though he was really his grandchild.

Brought up as a prince, with the passing of the years, Moses proved to be a man of great value, and when the Ethiopians invaded Egypt, devastating the countryside all the way up to Memphis, it was the priests who advised putting Moses at the head of the Egyptian army.

Moses led his troops, not down the side of the Nile where his enemies would be expecting him, but across the desert to outflank them. Josephus comments that the desert was a highly dangerous place because it teemed with snakes "of terrible strength, wickedness and size," and that there were flying snakes, reptiles that attacked from the sky.

However, the astute commander had already thought of this and was taking with him an entire caravan of cages filled with ibises, "birds that were the natural predators of snakes" and, when they reached the dangerous region, the soldiers let the ibis free. Flying ahead of the army, they cleared the path of everything wriggling on the ground. Thus the Egyptian army fell upon the unsuspecting Ethiopians and routed them. They fled back to Ethiopia and holed up in the capital of Saba (later renamed Meroë), which Moses surrounded and besieged. The city held out for a long time as it was protected by fast rivers, banks and high walls. But the affair came to an unexpected conclusion when the lovely Ethiopian princess Tharbis, "seeing Moses fighting with great valor and admiring his well planned tactics," fell in love with him and proposed a marriage between the two that would seal a peace. He accepted the proposal, the marriage was held in Saba and then he returned to Egypt as a successful general and husband.

The biblical account of Moses' life ignores his childhood, this warring episode and his Ethiopian wife, and only tells us that, one day, having come across an Egyptian who was beating a Jew, he killed him and buried the body in the sand. The pharaoh came to hear of it and sentenced Moses to death, whereupon Moses left Egypt and hid in the land of Midian, whose inhabitants were also the descendants of Abraham.

Nomads whose existence was based on grazing, the Midianites lived on both sides of what is today the Gulf of Aqaba, which separates the Sinai Peninsula from the Arab coast. During his flight, Moses stopped by a well to rest but was obliged to defend seven girls drawing water for their flock from shepherds who tried to drive them away to water their own animals. The girls were the daughters of Reuel, the priest of Midian, whose title was Jethro ("Your Excellence'"). The girls took Moses to their father's camp where he was made guardian of the flocks and was given the eldest daughter, Zipporah, as his wife. Together they had two sons, Gershom and Eleazar.

90 and 91 Domenico Fetti's early 18th-century painting of
Moses and the Burning *Bush* shows the leader as an ordinary
man. Fetti's work reveals many influences, for example,
Rubens and the Venetian school, whereas in Rosso Fiorentino's
painting of Moses and Jethro's Daughters *(right)*, we note a
strong plasticity in the figures reminiscent of Michelangelo.

The Burning Bush

Moses was forty years old when he left Egypt, and he remained with the Midianites for another forty. Then the Lord appeared to him because, in the meantime, the pharaoh (thought to be Seti I) had died and the Jews had called for divine help against his successor (thought to be Ramesses II) who persecuted them in their bondage. One day, leading Reuel's flocks to pasture in the Sinai, Moses was struck by a strange sight, one of the thorny bushes that grow among the rocks appeared to be in flames though it did not burn. He approached and heard a solemn, mysterious voice ordering him to remove his shoes as the ground on which he stood was holy. "I am the God of Abraham, the God of Isaac and the God of Jacob," the voice said, and Moses fell to his knees and covered his face with fear. The Lord told Moses that he was to free his people from bondage in Egypt and lead them to the land of "milk and honey."

(Moses was astonished and reluctant, as he felt he was inadequate for such a task, but God promised him help and demonstrated the power he would have by turning his staff into a snake. This staff was to be taken to Egypt and used in front of the pharaoh to perform miracles.

92 One of the most common episodes in Christian art, the revelation of God in the form of the burning bush, marked Moses' vocation and the beginning of his mission. Top, a version by Fra Eustachio (Tommaso di Baldassare, 1473-1555) in an illuminated letter from the early 16th century, and bottom, Raphael's interpretation in the Vatican Loggias.

93 top In AD 327, St. Helena, the mother of Emperor
Constantine, had a chapel dedicated to the Virgin Mary
built in the Sinai desert at the place she believed Moses
saw the burning bush. Over the centuries, the construction
of St. Catherine's monastery increasingly enclosed the chapel.

93 bottom St. Catherine's monastery, which is still inhabited by
an Orthodox community, stands at the end of a narrow valley
on the north side of Mount Sinai. It is protected by natural
and manmade defenses and has survived so long owing to
the respect that the holiness of the site has always inspired.

94-95 Thanks to generous donations, St. Catherine's monastery was already substantially developed just three centuries after its foundation. A request was made to Emperor Justinian to fortify the site to defend it from Bedouin raids; the red granite walls that surround it date

95 The monastery's most important well is Bir Musa ('Moses' Well') to the right of the entrance. Tradition has it that this is where Moses met Jethro's daughters, including his future wife Zipporah. The Basilica of the Transfiguration, the heart of the group of buildings,

St. Catherine's Monastery

During the Christian era, in the year 327, with the help of divine grace, St. Helena, the mother of the Roman emperor Constantine (who adopted Christianity as the religion of the empire), identified the place where God had spoken to Moses. Around the spot where the burning bush had stood, she had a monastery built that was dedicated to St. Catherine. The story of Catherine was that, after she was martyred in Alexandria, angels spirited her body to the top of Mount Sinai. In the mid-6th century the Byzantine emperor Justinian fortified the monastery against raids by the Bedouin, and today the building is still standing on the slopes of the mountain, a little island of Orthodox Christianity in a Moslem land. It has been protected since the Arab conquest by a doc-

God will free the Israelites

Obedient to God's will, Moses returned to Memphis and presented himself before the king with his brother Aaron. The two octogenarians first implored the pharaoh (probably Ramesses II or his son Merenptah) to let the Jews free, and then threatened him, but the king of Upper and Lower Egypt refused to let them leave Egypt. God punished the stubborn ruler by sending ten 'plagues.' Each was more terrible than the former. The water of the Nile turned to blood; there was a plague of frogs, then lice, then flies; Egyptian herds and flocks died (but not those of Israel); the people suffered from a plague of boils; and hail was sent that destroyed crops and trees; and swarms of locusts were sent across Egypt to devour what was left of the crops. Yet the king refused to let the Jews go even when Egypt was covered by darkness for three days. He only gave in when God's anger put the firstborn of every family and animal to death, but not those of the Israelites.

96 This scene in the Ramesseum shows Ramesses II fighting the forces of Amurru during the Syrian campaign in the eighth to tenth years of his reign (1271-70 BC). The image of the war chariot attacking the enemy suggests how determined the pharaoh was to harass the Jews.

97 Michelangelo's Moses includes one of the most curious features in the iconography of the prophet: the horns on his head. These result from a mistake in the Latin translation from the Hebrew: the 'rays of light' that emanated from Moses' face after his descent from Mount Sinai were translated into 'golden horns' and have remained as such.

The Ten Plagues of Egypt

98 and 99 top *The first Egyptian plague turned the water of the Nile to blood, as illustrated left in the* Bible Historiale *by Guiard des Moulins (late 13th century), and, top, taken from the 'Mozarabic' Bible produced in Moorish Spain in the 10th century. Mozarabic art also developed in Sicily at about the same rate as pre-Romanesque, and came to an end around 1100.*

99 center *Some of the Egyptian plagues (ulcers and hail, left; locusts and darkness, right) are shown here in the Jewish artistic tradition, taken from the famous Shealtiel Haggadah. This is a 14th-century illuminated manuscript in Catalan style, now in the British Museum. The word* haggadah *means 'story' and the Haggadah shel Pesach is the text read at the Jewish Passover (Pesach).*

Crossing the Red Sea

Finally, an immense column of Jews set out, with their flocks and herds, and jewels of silver and gold and fine raiment that the Egyptians had given in accordance with the promise of the Lord as recompense for their suffering. They left the city of Ramesses and headed southeast to Succoth, then to Etam on the Bitter Lakes. Here they heard that the pharaoh had changed his mind and had sent his army to follow them, thus they altered direction and moved north, flanking the marshes through which, many centuries later, the Suez Canal was dug. This area was the Sea of Reeds near Baal-zephon, a quagmire that an error of interpretation in the Greek version of the Old Testament translated as the Red Sea. Here the waters receded at the touch of Moses' staff to let the Jews cross, but not the Egyptian army, which was engulfed by the returning waters when they attempted to follow the Jews across the narrow passage that had been opened.

100-101 This map is taken from Voyage des Enfan[t]s d'Israel dans le Desert depuis leur Sortie d'Egypte par la Mer Rouge jusques au Pays de Canaan, *published in Amsterdam in 1690 by Pieter Mortier. It shows the wanderings of the children of the God of Israel, with close reference to the accounts given in the Books of Exodus and Numbers, until the crossing of the River Jordan narrated in the Book of Joshua.*

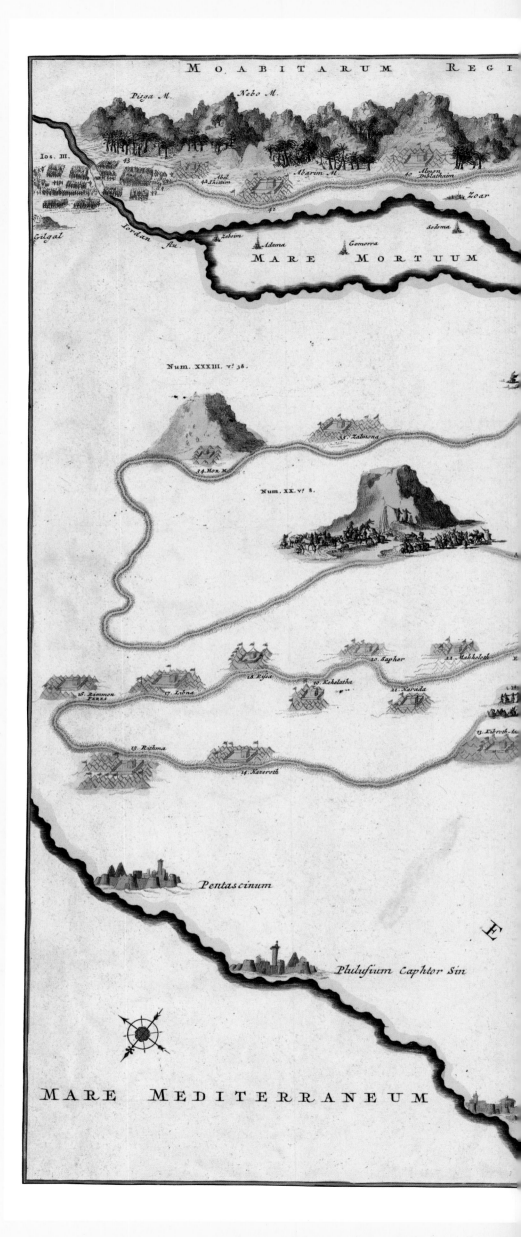

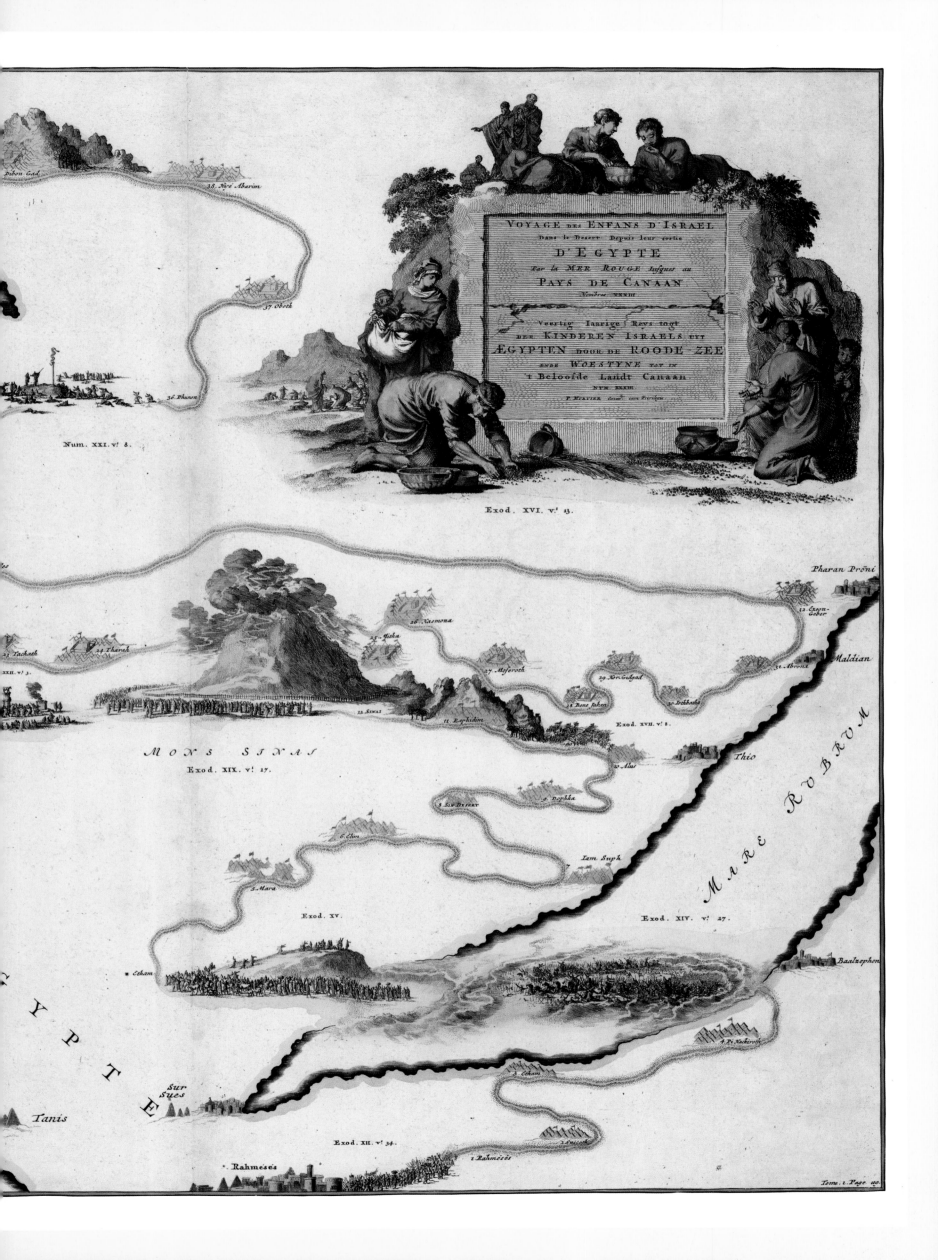

VOYAGE DES ENFANS D'ISRAEL
Dans le Desert Depuis leur sortie
D'EGYPTE
Par la MER ROUGE Iusques au
PAYS DE CANAAN
Nombres XXXIII

Veertig Iaurige Reys togt
DER KINDEREN ISRAELS UYT
ÆGYPTEN DOOR DE ROODE ZEE
ENDE WOESTYNE TOT IN
t Beloofde Landt Canaan
NUM XXIII
P. MORTIER Excud: cum Privilegio

Dibon-Gad

38. Ieié Abarim

37. Oboth

Num. XXI. v! 8.   36. Phunon

Exod. XVI. v! 13.

Pharan Proni

12. Ezeon-Geber

26. Rasmona

25. Hitka   31. Abrona   Maldian

23. Tachath   24. Tharah   27. Meseroth

XXII. v! 3.   29. Ion-Gilgad

                                                 28. Bene Iakan   30. Iethbatha

                                    12. SINAI   11. Raphidim   Exod. XVII. v! 8.

MONS   SINAI

Exod. XIX. v! 17.   Thio

                                               10. Alus

                                          9. Dophka

                         8. Sur Desert

              6. Elim

                                                                    MARE   RVBRVM

                                          Iam Suph

5. Mara

Exod. XV.   Exod. XIV. v! 27.

* Etham   Baalzephon

                                                              4. Pi Nachiroth

                                               3. Etham

Sur
Sues

Tanis   2. Succoth

Exod. XII. v! 34.

* Rahmeses   1. Rahmeses

EGYPTE   Tome. 1. Page 110.

Crossing the Red Sea

102 and 103 The crossing of the Red Sea is one of the most frequently illustrated episodes from the Bible. In this late 16th century painting, the painter and engraver Antonio Tempesta treats the theme with his typical liveliness and technical precision. The rendition of the mountains in the distance is a faithful representation of the geological formations on the coast of the Red Sea, almost as if the artist had visited the region.

God provides his people with food

Having crossed to the western edges of the Desert of Sur, the migrating Jews were safe. However, instead of heading straight to Canaan (the land God had promised them), they turned south down the Gulf of Suez following Moses' sister, Miriam, and other women who danced to the sound of the timbrels in joy.

After three months of hardship in the desolate wilderness of Elim and Sin, where only divine intervention saved them from starvation by sending them a flock of quails and raining manna down upon them, the people of Israel camped by the slopes of Mount Sinai.

104 This illumination by Belbello of Pavia is taken from the 15th-century Landau-Finaly codex. It shows Moses causing water to flow from a rock in one of the many supernatural phenomena that occurred during the wanderings of the Israelites in the desert.

105 In this lovely Czech painting in the Gothic style (1480-1490), the episode of the miraculous spring is shown with that of the manna from heaven.

Moses and the Ten Commandments

The mountain smoked and trembled as God called Moses to speak with him on the peak. Moses climbed to the top several times and finally received the stone tablets on which the Ten Commandments were carved. But during Moses' long absence, the Israelites below had been corrupted and convinced Moses' weak brother Aaron to melt down their jewelry and cast a golden calf to worship as an idol. When Moses saw this on his return, he smashed the tablets with anger and flung the idol into the fire. Repentant, the Jews returned to worship the true God, and Moses asked for divine pardon for the people. God provided Moses with two new tablets and the pact between the Lord and the people of Israel was reconfirmed.

In spring, the caravan continued on its way towards the Promised Land, flanking the Gulf of Aqaba and then turning north toward Canaan. Priests marched at the head of the caravan, bearing the Ark of the Covenant. This was a portable altar made from a box of acacia wood lined with gold; it contained the tablets of the Law, Aaron's staff that had performed miracles in Egypt and the desert, and some of the manna that had rained down upon them from heaven. Above the Covenant of the Ark, the Holy Spirit hovered gently in the form of a cloud during the day and like a column of fire by night. The people of Israel followed, drawn up in the twelve tribes established by Jacob. After they left the desert of Sin the Jews journeyed north through Rephidim and later camped near Kadesh-barnea on the edge of Canaan, where they found water and grazing land.

108-109 These illuminations are from a manuscript dating from 1300-25 with text – a moral compendium – written by the confessor of King Philip III of France, who reigned from 1270 to 1285. Left, Moses receives the Ten Commandments; right, three trumpeters next to the golden calf, protected by a Gothic-style pavilion.

Toward Canaan

Before entering Canaan itself en masse, twelve men were sent ahead to reconnoiter, who returned after forty days saying that it was truly the land of milk and honey, and, as proof, showed an enormous bunch of grapes. But they also said that the inhabitants were enormous, like giants, in comparison with whom they felt as small as locusts, and claimed that the country was unconquerable: the cities were too well-defended and the men too strong. Two of the twelve – Joshua and Caleb – were not so pessimistic, and had faith in the divine promise, but the majority of the Israelites despaired and cried out with sorrow at having left Egypt. Then the Lord once more became angry against this unruly people and punished them with a further forty days wandering in the Negev. When Moses judged that they had suffered enough, they began their march north once more, but passed through Edom (southern Jordan) to the east. Here, Aaron died. He was buried on top of a mountain that the Bible refers to as Hor and which, traditionally, is identified with Jebel Harun (meaning "the mountain of Aaron" in Arabic).

But the Edomites refused to let the enormous caravan pass, likewise the Moabites to the north of Edom, so the Jews were obliged to make the long and exhausting journey around their kingdoms. When they once more turned west to cross the land of the Amorites, they had to defeat the forces of King Sihon so they might pass, and this and other victories against the Midianites gave the people of Israel the land to the east of Jordan. By now 120 years old, Moses had concluded his superhuman task as his people were now just a step from Canaan. He gathered them at the foot of Mount Nebo and made three long speeches on the laws that had been established to govern Israel, then he climbed the mountain in accordance with the will of God and was shown the Promised Land before closing his eyes forever. According to tradition, Archangel Michael came down from heaven to bury Moses' body in a secret place.

112 bottom This enameled plaque was decorated using the champlevé technique. It comes from a cross made in the Meuse in France in the 12th century and shows two of the twelve men sent to reconnoiter Canaan carrying back an enormous bunch of grapes as proof of the fertility of the land.

Victory over the Amorites

114-115 The Jews head toward the Promised Land as they fight against King Sihon. Around 1624 Nicolas Poussin (1594-1665), one of the greatest 17th century French artists, painted Joshua's Victory over the Amorites. Shortly after, owing to financial problems, the artist was forced to sell this magnificent picture for a tiny sum. Today it is in the Pushkin Museum, Moscow.

16-117 *The large fresco of the* Testament and Death of
Moses in the Sistine Chapel – in which Luca Signorelli
undoubtedly painted some of the figures – depicts a theme
frequently seen in the mosaics of the early Middle Ages
and illuminations in biblical codices.

THE LAND OF MILK AND HONEY

118 *Led by Joshua, the people of Israel prepare to cross the River Jordan. Curiously, the figures are shown from behind; ahead is the city they aim to reach, whose 15th-century-style towers can be seen in the distance. From a 15th century Flemish illuminated codex in the Musée Condé, Chantilly, France.*

119 *This illumination from the Maciejowski Bible (in the copy in the Morgan Library, New York) illustrates the first part of the Old Testament – from Genesis to the history of King David. This page shows episodes from the life of Samson in his struggle against the Philistines. Note the unusual scene top right, in which the hero tears down the gates of Gaza to escape.*

The crossing of the River Jordan

azing across the Jordan valley from the top of Mount Nebo, Moses had seen an expanse of orchards, fields, woods and grazing land on which flocks of sheep and goats wandered. Vines, olives, figs, dates, walnuts, pistachios, carob trees, sycamores, poplars, tamarisks and oaks studded the landscape. Much earlier, the fertility of this land had struck an Egyptian prince who had crossed it when Canaan belonged to the pharaohs, and he described it as follows: "It is a very wonderful land. There are figs and broad beans, there is more wine than water; there is plenty of honey, an infinity of oil and every sort of fruit. There is barley and spelt; the land teems with livestock. Every day they prepared bread for me, they brought me wine, meat, poultry and game in abundance."

This land had been divided into a number of small states, with each governed by a king, after Egypt's sovereignty had been overthrown. The

Canaanites lived and prospered, worshiping the sun, the moon, the stars and a number of 'cruel and infamous' gods like Baal, Astarte, Moloch and Chamos to whom they made human sacrifices. It was this evil that had roused the anger of the Lord and convinced him to allot the country to the Jews as punishment. The Bible states several times that this dispossession was decreed on high. Joshua, the new leader of the Chosen People was eighty-five years old when preparations were made for the conquest of the Promised Land. He had gained experience while under Moses' command and shown great skills, courage, wisdom and intelligence. It was he who turned to the Lord when the moment came: "Arise. Go over this Jordan, thou and all this people, unto the land which I do give to them, even to the children of Israel ... There shall not any man be able to stand before thee all the days of thy life: as I was with Moses, so I shall be with thee: I will not fail thee nor forsake thee. Do not be

afraid, neither be thou dismayed, for the Lord thy God is with thee whithersoever thou goest." Joshua had complete faith in this promise.

The Jews were camped in the plain of Moab, a few miles from the city of Jericho, which lay on the other side of the river Jordan. Jericho was the key to the central region and controlled the north-south roads that ran along the foot of the grayish limestone mountains called Gebel Karantal. Jericho was referred to as "the city of palm groves" or "the paradise of Canaan" because it was surrounded by a well-irrigated plain covered with vegetation. But, as Biblical commentators were to write, "its corruption equaled its splendor." In short, Jericho was another

of the Jews had performed extraordinary feats, such as parting the "Red Sea" and making possible the Jews' victory over the Amorites. She could not but believe that such a powerful God had to be the one true God of heaven and earth. This act of faith won her the posthumous praise of St. Paul as well as marriage to a prince of the tribe of Judah, and thus made her the ancestor of David and the Messiah.

The two spies climbed down from Rahab's roof over the city walls and returned to Joshua to report that the inhabitants of the whole city trembled at the name of the Jews. At this, the entire people – not an army – set off to cross the Jordan; more than a military advance, it was a religious procession. The Ark

120 and 121 Scenes from the Old Testament form an important cycle of mosaics in the Basilica of Santa Maria Maggiore, Rome. The two sections shown here illustrate episodes from the Book of Joshua: left, the crossing of the River Jordan, and right, the sending of scouts to Jericho when Rahab (from the top of the wall) informs the king's emissaries that the two men have already left. These and other scenes from Exodus, Numbers and Joshua focus on God's help to the Chosen People during their long journey to the Promised Land.

Sodom and was to suffer the same fate. Although Joshua had every confidence in his divine protection, before attacking the fortified city he took precautions. He sent two young men to explore, who, after six hours march, entered Jericho where they stayed in the house of a prostitute and inn-keeper named Rahab. She was a sinner with a good heart for, when the inhabitants of the city heard of the two strangers in their midst, they thought them rightly to be Jewish spies and informed their king. The king's soldiers were sent to arrest the pair but Rahab hid them under the flax on the roof of her house and told the guards the men had already left. The guards hastened off in the direction of the Jordan, hoping to catch the pair, but to no avail. As a precaution, the king had the gates of the city closed.

Meanwhile, Rahab explained to the two men why she had saved their lives. Like everyone, the inhabitants of Jericho had heard the stories of how the God

of the Covenant was carried solemnly before the column of Jews at a distance of two thousand cubits (about a thousand yards) and God in person opened the way toward Canaan. As it was spring, the melted snows in the mountains had filled the river and the water flowed quickly, but as soon as the bearers of the Ark arrived at the riverbank, the current came to a halt. The waters flowing down from upstream were halted leaving the riverbed dry so that the priests with the Ark and the host could pass over the river with dry feet.

When they had all reached the other bank, the priests who had halted with the Ark in the center of the riverbed also passed over and the water began to flow once more. But on the first side Joshua had had his people build a rudimentary monument of twelve stones and had another twelve – one for each tribe – carried across to the Canaanite side where they were placed to commemorate the miracle for all time.

The fall of Jericho

This was the place named Gilgal, which lay halfway between the Jordan and Jericho, and was the site of a later city where pilgrims during the Middle Ages were still shown the twelve stones. Here the Jews set up their camp and gave themselves over to religious celebrations. All those who had not yet been circumcised were circumcised, and they celebrated the Passover, which was a service that during their wanderings they had been able to observe only at the foot of Mount Sinai.

Once purified, the Jews were ready to take Jericho, but before they could advance, Joshua saw before him a man with his sword drawn in his hand who declared that he was the "captain of the host of the Lord." He had come to deliver Jericho, its king and people into the hands of the Jews. The instructions of God were that the Jews should march around the walls of the city in perfect silence for six days. The inhabitants would watch them from the walls, frightened by the mysterious spectacle. Then, on the seventh day, the Ark would be carried forward by seven priests who would blow the rams' horn trumpets to create eerie, menacing music.

For seven days the Jews did as they were bid, circling the city walls, then, as ordered by Joshua, when the trumpets sounded they all shouted in unison and the massive walls of Jericho crumbled to the ground. The Jewish warriors entered the city and killed every man, woman and child except for Rahab and her family; they were saved because of the help they had given the Jews. Jericho was burned and an immense booty of gold, silver and bronze was given to the priests so that they could honor God.

122 Guiard des Moulins' Bible Historiale (late 13th century) shows a figure with unsheathed sword appearing to Joshua before the walls of Jericho. The figure portrayed is an angel with turquoise wings, a characteristic added to the story under artistic license during the Middle Ages.

123 *Soldiers armed with spears and shields attack the*
famous and ancient walls of Jericho. At the sounds of the
trumpets and war cries of the Jews, the walls begin to
crumble. This dramatic moment described in Joshua 6,
20 was painted in the Vatican Loggias by followers of
Raphael.

Stop, O Sun!

Joshua cursed the city and whoever tried to rebuild it. During the time of Achab, the impious Hiel of Bethel wanted to rebuild Jericho on its ruins. His eldest son was killed when he laid the foundations; his youngest son was killed when he placed the city gates in position. It is not known how long this second cursed city lasted, but it was no longer there when Mark Antony gave the district to Cleopatra, who wished for it so she could scheme against Herod the Great.

Herod the Great built a third Jericho to the south

too far gone for him to win a victory over his enemies. So he asked God to halt the sun's journey: "And the sun stood still and the moon stayed … and the sun hasted not to go down for a whole day. And there was no day like it before it or after it … for the Lord fought for Israel."

In an attempt to reconcile religious faith with astronomy, pious 19th-century commentators timidly proposed that there had been an optical illusion, a purely local refraction of light. However it was, Joshua had the time to rout the Amorites,

124 The Maciejowski Bible is also known as the 'Crusaders' Bible' because of the knights' surcoats which resemble medieval armored tunics. Joshua is shown at the top fighting the king of the Amorites, while, below, the defeated kings are tracked down to a cave near Makkeda and dishonored.

125 In an episode taken from the Story of Joshua in the Vatican, the leader of the Israelites asks the Sun and Moon to halt on their paths. According to some, this cycle of frescoes reveals the hand of Perin del Vaga, one of Raphael's favorite pupils who, in 1520, collaborated on the decoration of the Loggias.

126-127 This map drawn by Abraham bar Yaakov in about 1695 was one of the first annotated in Hebrew. It shows the route of the Jews during the Exodus and the division of the tribes of Israel. The pictures round the edge are symbolic: the honeycombs beneath a portico, left, and the four head of cattle represent the fertility of the Promised Land, while the eagle alludes to divine power and the woman on a crocodile to Africa. Also seen is the episode of Jonah in the whale and the voyage of Solomon's ships to Lebanon to bring back cedars to build the Temple.

of the original city with palaces, gardens, theaters and a circus, and made it his winter residence. He died in this city, which had become the point where Jewish pilgrims from Perea and Galilee met on their way to the Temple in Jerusalem. Jesus too visited it, as we shall see.

After the fall of Jericho, the Jews took the rest of Canaan in a series of military victories with the help of an even more spectacular miracle. When the forces of Israel had come to the aid of the city of Gibeon (which had allied itself with Israel and been attacked by a confederation of five Amorite kings), Joshua realized during the battle that the day was

and to chase the five kings to a cave near the city of Makkedah, where they were captured and hanged from five trees. The rest of the Book of Joshua reads like a war journal, listing the lands conquered and their division among the tribes of Israel. The leader of the Chosen People was given a city all to himself: Timnath-serah in the region of the tribe of Ephraim. It was here that he died at the age of 110, after ordering the removal of the Tabernacle and the Ark to Silo (Seilun) on the top of a hill. This town was for the first three centuries the religious center of the Chosen People and a place of pilgrimage for all twelve tribes.

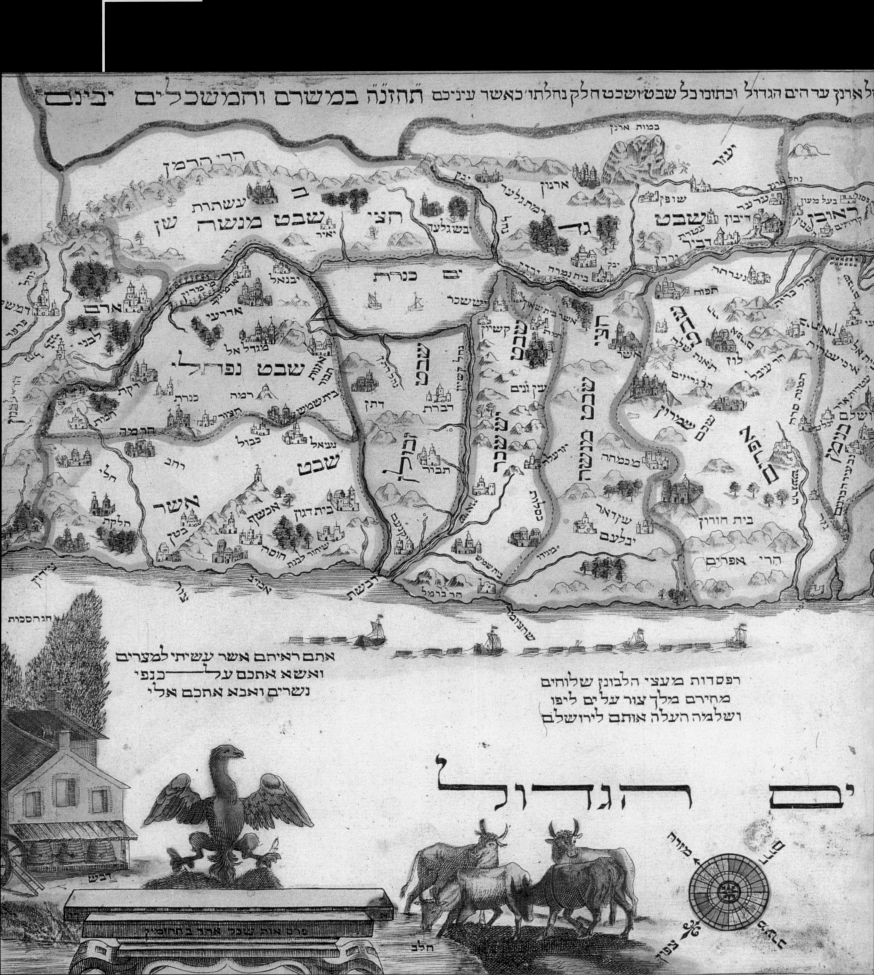

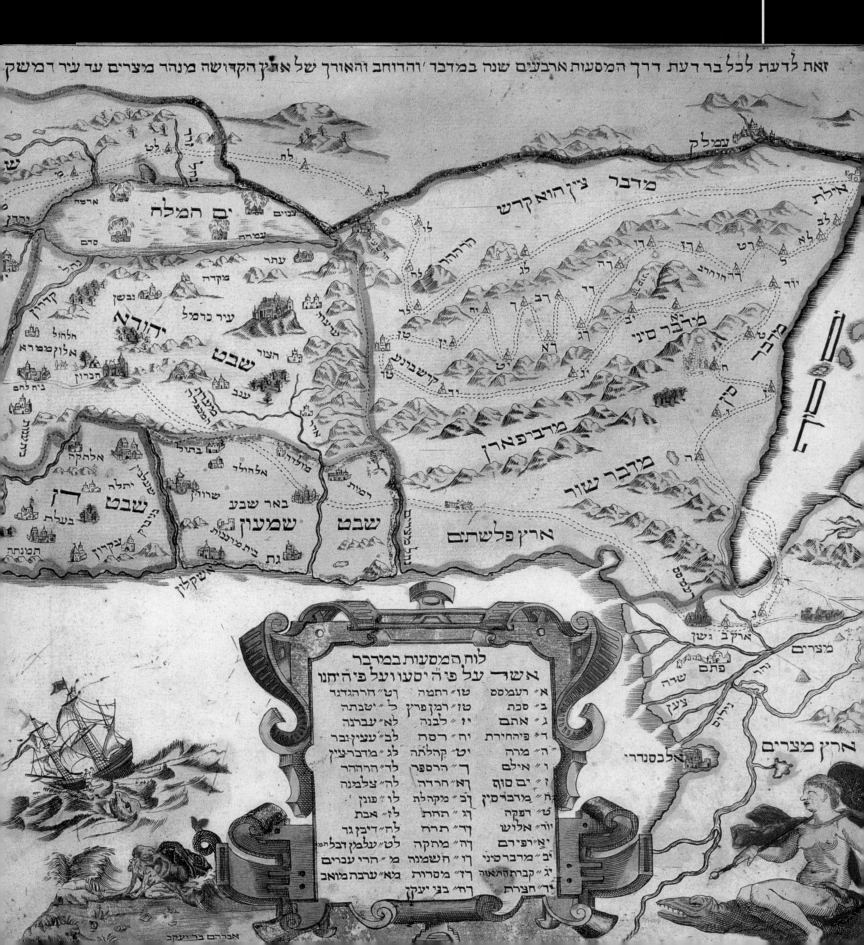

זאת לדעת לכל בר דעת דרך המסעות ארבעים שנה במדבר 'והרוחב והאורך של א"ץ הקדושה מנהר מצרים עד עיר דמשק

עמלק

מדבר צין הוא קדש

אלת

מדבר סיני

ים המלח

יהודה

שבט

עיר כרמל

שבט שמעון

שבט דן

ארץ פלשתים

מדבר שור

מדבר פאראן

הים הגדול

מצרים

פתם

ארץ מצרים

אלכסנדרי

לוח המסעות במדבר
אשר על פי ה' יסעו ועל פי ה' יחנו

טו" רתמה	א" רעמסס
טז" רמן פרץ	ב" סכת
יז" לבנה	ג" אתם
יח" רסה	ד" פי החירת
יט" קהלתה	ה" מרה
ך" הר ספר	ו" אילם
כא" חרדה	ז" ים סוף
כב" מקהלת	ח" מדבר סין
כג" תחת	ט" רפקה
כד" תרח	יו" אלוש
כה" מתקה	יא" רפידים
כו" חשמנה	יב" מדבר סיני
כז" מסרות	יג" קברת התאוה
כח" בני יעקן	יד" חצרות

וט" חר הגדגד
ל" יטבתה
לא" עברנה
לב" עצין גבר
לג" מדבר צין
לד" הר ההר
לה" צלמנה
לו" פונן
לז" אבת
לח" דיבן גד
לט" עלמן דבלת"
מ" הרי עברים
מא" בארבת מואב

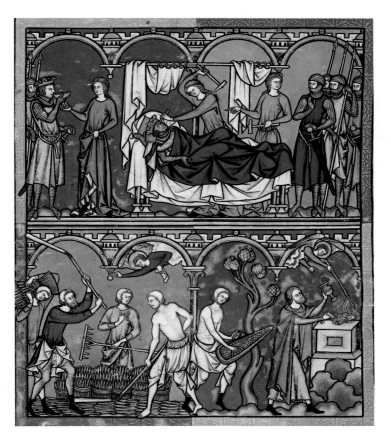

The war continued even after Joshua's death as parts of Canaan were still in the hands of the Canaanites, who bitterly resisted. It was then that the Jews took the city of Jerusalem, then Hebron where, according to Josephus, "there still lived groups of giants, who, for the size of their bodies and their features, completely different to all other men, were strange to see and terrible to hear." And he added that in his time their bones could still be seen. This time marked the beginning of the period of the "judges," a word that referred to the captains of the people of Israel who, chosen directly at irregular intervals by God, completed the conquest of Canaan or led the Israelites against the invasions of foreigners. Their duties were basically military and their command temporary. When one of these judges, Gideon, was offered the royal crown, he refused it saying that the Jews were not born to serve a king on earth but only God.

The Bible talks little of some of these judges but more about others, for example, Deborah the prophetess who, though a woman, "judged Israel" beneath a palm tree between Ramah and Beth-el on Mount Ephraim. As had occurred on other occasions, the Chosen People had fallen into sin and the Lord had punished them by allowing them to be defeated and oppressed for twenty years by the Canaanite king Jabin, who had 300,000 soldiers, 10,000 horsemen and 900 iron chariots.

When the Jews had suffered enough for God to take pity on them once more, He inspired Deborah to call a warrior named Barak to her and gather together a force to free Israel from the yoke. Barak camped at the foot of Mount Tabor with Deborah and his army of 10,000 men, but when his troops saw the immense army under the leadership of Sisera approach, they trembled with fear. Then Deborah promised them victory in the name of the Lord and inflamed them with holy ardor so that they rushed down on the Canaanites and fought them in the plain of Esdraelon or Jezreel. This site is also known as Megiddo, and was the scene of many battles before and later, including those under Pharaoh Ramesses II and Napoleon.

Despite their overwhelming number, Sisera's soldiers could not win as God sent down violent rain and hail that blinded them. Worse was to follow when the rainstorm filled the River Chison that ran across the plain and washed away the Canaanites. The Arabs still call the river Nahr el Muqatta (River of the Massacre). And Sisera found himself alone as all his men had been cut down or had fled. He too tried to escape, so climbed down from his chariot and walked to the village of Cades where he found refuge in the tent of Heber the Kenite. Heber's wife Jael pretended to welcome him and hide him beneath a carpet but her sympathies were with Israel, though she was a Canaanite, not an Israelite, and when Sisera fell asleep, she took a nail from the tent and hammered it into his temple and down into the ground. When Barak arrived in pursuit, he found his enemy lying in his own blood.

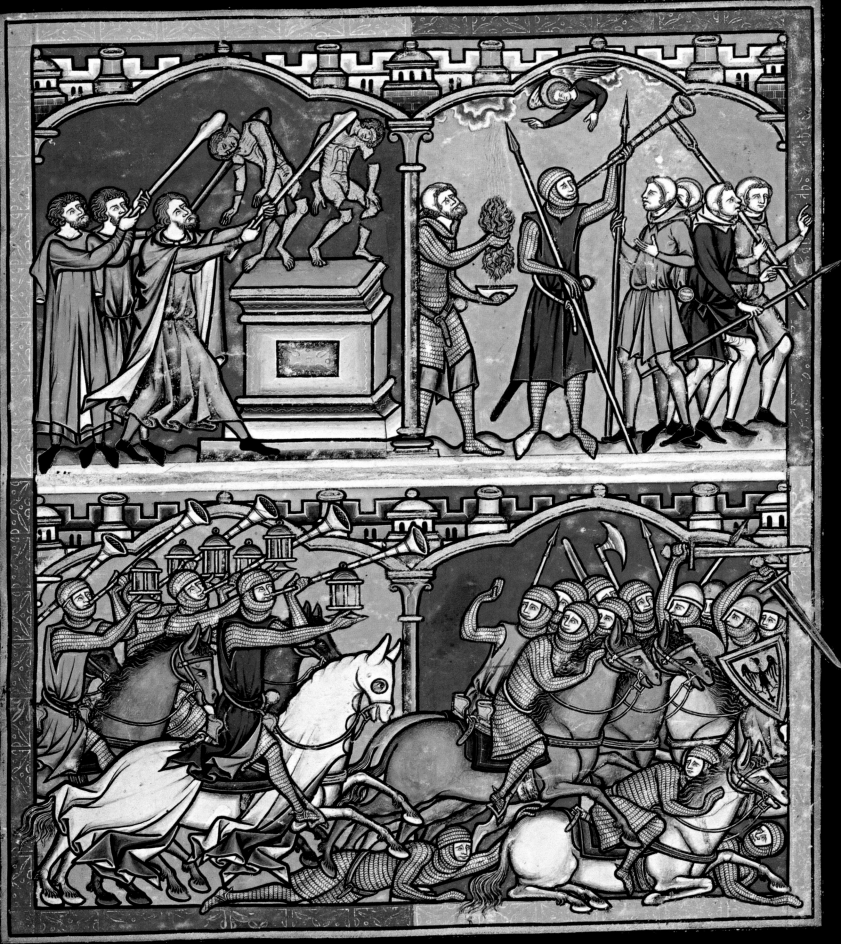

The Sea Peoples

But even though the Jews had liberated themselves from the Canaanites, "the children of Israel did evil in the sight of the Lord' once more, perhaps because they once more turned to idolatry, and thus drew down on themselves yet another retribution. This time the punishment was at the hands of the Midianites, who lived to the east of the River Jordan. For seven consecutive years they and the Amalekites and the Arabs invaded the lands of the Israelites, sacking and devastating until the inhabitants were forced to abandon the indefensible plains and take to the mountains. Finally, they implored the Lord for help and He chose a new judge called Gideon from the tribe of Manasseh, who was informed of his holy task by an angel as he worked in the fields.

God provided yet another manifestation of his power when the Midianites and their allies were camped on the edge of the plain of Megiddo on the slopes of Mount Moreh. They filled the western end of the valley "like grasshoppers for multitude, and their camels were without number, as the sand by the

sea side for multitude." Gideon camped on the flank of Mount Gilead with his 32,000 men, whereas his enemy had an army of 130,000, but the Lord told Gideon that his army was too large and that the "fearful and afraid" should leave; this left 10,000. Too many still, said the Lord, take them down to the water and send away all those who kneel and "lappeth of the water with his tongue, as a dog lappeth." This left just 300 men – who drank the water from a cupped hand – and it was with these that Gideon attacked the Midianites at night. He divided his group into three companies and gave each man a trumpet and a pitcher and a lamp within each pitcher. They crept up to the enemy camp and, at the order from Gideon, they blew their trumpets and broke the pitchers that they held so that the lights all became visible together. Confusion and panic broke out amongst the Midianites and they started to fight one another, while those that

escaped and tried to cross the Jordan were cut down by the Jews of Ephraim, who came down the mountain at Gideon's call.

Following this massacre, Gideon governed Israel for a further forty years but refused to let himself be crowned. But nonetheless the children of Israel continued to displease the Lord. Other punishments were meted out and other judges placed over them in a continual cycle until the Lord "gave them up to the hands of the Philistines for forty years."

Called by the Egyptians the 'Sea Peoples," the Philistines may have come from the island of Crete to the eastern Mediterranean hoping eventually to conquer Egypt and her riches. Chased out in 1188 BC by Ramesses III, they had settled along the coast of Canaan, which was named Palestine after them. There they founded a confederation of five cities: Ekron, Ashdod, Ashkelon, Gat and the most important, Gaza. And "they lorded over Israel."

The coming of the umpteenth savior was announced by an angel to a woman that the Bible does not name, however, she was the wife of an important man named Manoah in the tribe of Dan. Prophesying the birth of a son, the divine messenger told the woman not to drink wine or impure food, nor to cut the child's hair because the Lord would miraculously invest the child with superhuman strength represented by his hair.

The son was called Samson. He grew blessed by God and, when he was a man, "the spirit of the Lord began to move him." One day he went from his birthplace Saras, which overlooked the coastal plain, to the village of Timnath, where he saw a young Philistine girl who took his fancy. Despite his parents' opposition (mixed marriages were against the spirit of Israelite law), he asked them to go and request the girl for him as his wife.

When his father and mother set off on their disagreeable task, Samson accompanied them but "among the vines" as he was a morose and solitary person.

130 In this illumination from the Maciejowski Bible, God has ordered Gideon to demolish the altar of Baal that his father built, then to sound the trumpets and gather the people together to fight the Midianites. A man to Gideon's left holds out the lambskin with which he intends to test God's will by leaving it out for two nights under the dew. When the skin absorbs all the moisture, leaving the ground dry, Gideon has the signal that he has the Lord's support. The Midianites, bottom, will be defeated.

131 This 15th-century Flemish manuscript depicts the episode in Gideon's epic story when the Lord required him to take his men down to the river to drink, to decide who would attack the Midianites. Worried that the Israelites would ascribe victory to their numbers rather than divine assistance, God told Gideon to choose only those who drank from their hand without kneeling down by the water. Only 300 out of 10,000 passed the test.

Samson

As he journeyed, a lion attacked him but he killed it with his bare hands. When he passed by the animal again a few days later, he saw that a swarm of bees had built a nest in the animal's mouth, and he ate their honey. At the banquet set up to celebrate the marriage, there were thirty young Philistines to whom, as was customary, Samson set a riddle with a prize of thirty new sets of clothes and thirty tunics if it should be guessed. His riddle was, "Out of the eater came forth meat and out of the strong came forth sweetness." No one was able to guess the reference to the lion and the honey as Samson had not told anyone of the episode, but the Philistines wanted to win the bet and thus threatened Samson's new wife, who gave in and gave away the secret. When the Philistines triumphantly answered Samson's riddle, he understood his wife had told them. His anger knew no bounds. He went to Ashkelon where he killed thirty Philistines and took their clothes to pay off his debt; then he returned to his parents' village. Thinking herself repudiated, Samson's wife allowed herself to be remarried to one of the thirty Philistines, but Samson had not abandoned her and returned to take her to his house. When he discovered this second injury, he swore he would take vengeance on all Philistines.

132-133 Luca Giordano was a Neapolitan artist with a vivid imagination and prodigiously fast execution. In this interpretation, he shows Samson's fight with the lion as the

134 *This charcoal drawing by Tintoretto (1518-94) shows Samson, in a highly agitated state and with his arms and legs depicted under severe strain, massacring the Philistines. This people reached the coast of Palestine in the 13th century BC; they may have originated in Crete.*

135 *A thousand Philistines fell to the jawbone of an ass brandished by Samson in this dramatic work by Giorgio Schiavone, who was active in the second half of the 15th century. The most important artist from Dalmatia during the century, Schiavone signed himself Sclavonus ('Slav') in Italy, but his real name was Çulinoviç.*

With the coming of summer, he saw the corn of his enemies ripening in the sun, so he caught three hundred foxes, tied firebrands to their tails and let them run wild through the fields, setting all the corn, vineyards and olives on fire. In return the Philistines burned his wife and her father alive as they were guilty of causing this disaster. Then they set out to catch Samson. This marked the start of a war of attrition. Attacked by the Philistines, the leaders of the tribe of Judah implored Samson to give himself up. He agreed to let himself be handed over to his enemies with his hands bound, and the Philistines led him away triumphantly. But suddenly he snapped his the ropes and butchered a great number of them. He took the jawbone of an ass and used it to kill a thousand of the Philistines, then named the place where this slaughter took place Ramath-lehi (the Hill of the Jawbone), which lies to the northwest of Bethlehem. Here God caused water to gush from a rock to slake Samson's great thirst after such a battle.

Scornful of such weak enemies, Samson went straight to Gaza, the Philistines' capital, and stopped off at the house of a prostitute. Thinking they had him trapped, the Philistines shut the gates of the city but Samson got up in the middle of the night and lifted the gates and their posts clean out of the wall and carried them off up to a hill by Hebron.

His downfall was his love for a woman from the valley of Sorek called Delilah. When the Philistines learned of this relationship, the royal family offered her a large sum of money if she could learn the secret of Samson's superhuman strength. Three times Samson lied to Delilah, allowing himself to be bound by ropes that he broke easily. But the fourth time he confessed the truth of his hair, not knowing "that the Lord had departed from him." She made him sleep on her lap, then cut off his hair and called the Philistines. They took him, put out his eyes and transported him to Gaza where they made him turn a heavy mill in the prison. When, a short while later, the Philistine princes gathered in Gaza to make a sacrifice to Dagon, their god, they called for the blind Samson to be led out by a young girl to entertain them. What they did not realize was that in the meantime their prisoner's hair had grown back. Samson had himself led to between two pillars that held up the building, then called on the Lord to help him, and pushed against the pillars with all his refound strength. The building collapsed killing everyone in it. Samson's family recovered his body and buried next to his father Manoah, between the villages of Zorah and Eshtaol.

136 Captured by the Philistines, Samson is put in chains. Annibale Carracci, one of the principal artists in Rome in the early 17th century, was a member of an important family of Bolognese artists; here he portrays the mute desperation and humiliation of the imprisoned judge.

137 In the end Samson was brought down by a woman. Carlo Cignani (1628-1719), the standard bearer of Bolognese classicism, captures the moment when the young Delilah delicately takes a lock of Samson's hair and prepares to cut it.

KING SAUL AND DAVID

138 *The Westminster Psalter was compiled around 1200 to match Westminster Abbey's liturgy. It contains five full-page illuminations, the last of which shows David, crowned and enthroned like a medieval king, playing the harp. The Scriptures tell us that he was a skilled player whose music roused joy in his hearers.*

139 *The surprising statue of David armed with a sling in the Galleria Borghese in Rome was sculpted by Gian Lorenzo Bernini in 1623-24 for Cardinal Scipione Borghese. David's intensity, expressed through his sideways gaze, was based on Bernini's own intent face as he sculpted the marble.*

The struggle against the Philistines

After the death of Samson, the Jews recognized the high priest Eli as their leader. Israel's misfortunes were not yet finished: the Philistines lorded it over southern Canaan and one day their army advanced as far as Mizpeh. Here the Jews challenged the Philistines but were beaten, losing four thousand men. Then, without consulting the Lord, their leaders, believing they had lost divine favor and instead of analyzing the causes and attempting to put them right with prayer and penitence, decided to carry the Ark of the Covenant into their camp as though it were an infallible amulet. They sent to Shiloh to get it where it was in Eli's keeping. Being almost one hundred years old, Eli himself could not accompany the Ark so he sent his two sons.

At the sight of the Ark, the Jews shouted with joy and the Philistines from superstitious fear, but inciting themselves not to let themselves become the slaves of the Jews, the Philistines attacked with enthusiasm and overcame their enemy, killing thirty thousand. They also took possession of the Ark and when the venerable Eli heard the news, he fell from his seat, banged his head and died.

The triumphant Philistines carried their war booty to Ashdod, one of their five cities, and, as was customary throughout the Middle East, they placed it in the temple of Dagon, their fish-god and protector.

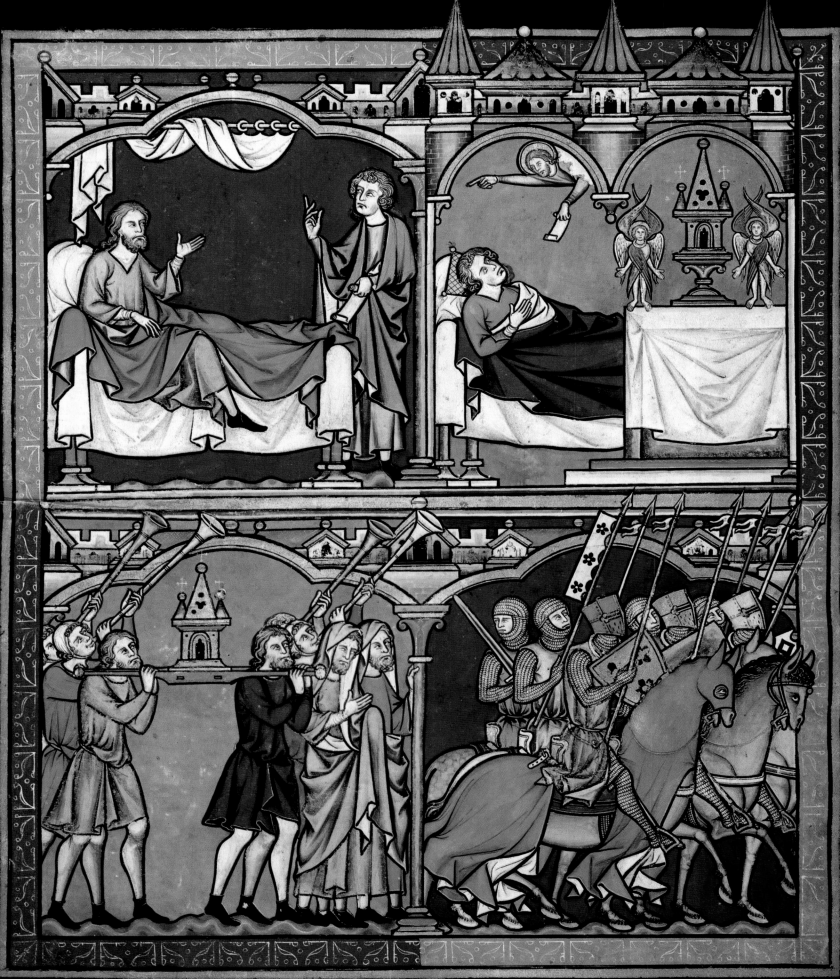

The scourges of God

But the Lord, though he had allowed the enemies of a fallen Israel to triumph, had no intention of allowing the dishonor to continue. The next day the priests who entered the temple found the statue of Dagon overturned in the dust. They righted it, but the next day it had fallen once more and this time the head and hands were broken.

Then the irascible god of Israel passed to more serious punishments: Ashdod was scourged by a painful and humiliating complaint which was probably hemorrhoids; then came an invasion of greedy rats that ate up the crops in the fields. Unlike the pharaoh of Egypt, the inhabitants of the city decided immediately to call for the help of their princes, who ordered the Ark to be removed to Gath. The convoy, however, was not in time to pass through the walls before all the inhabitants, 'from the youngest to the oldest,' were instantly struck by the complaint

represented the number of Philistine princes). They were to place them on a new cart drawn by two cows that had never been yoked before and which had each recently given birth to two calves. If the cows started walk off with the cart toward Israel unconcerned by the calls from their calves in the stalls, it would mean that the Ark had caused the calamity that had befallen the Philistines. The cows started off on the road to Beth-shemesh, which was the religious city built by the Jews on a hilltop about twelve miles away, and everyone in the town there was delighted to see it arrive. The cows stopped by a large stone on which the Ark was placed, then they were sacrificed on a fire made from the wood of the cart. But seventy of the Beth-shemites looked into the Ark from curiosity and the Lord did not pardon them, smiting them down. So the Jewish inhabitants of the town were now as fearful as the Philistines had been

142 This illumination from the Maciejowski Bible shows (top) the two punishments meted out to the city of Ashdod by God: a humiliating epidemic and a plague of rats. Bottom left, the arrival of the Ark at Beth-shemesh with the Levites who place it down on a large rock; right, a few head of cattle are sacrificed.

143 In the cathedral in Anagni, south of Rome, a 12th-13th century cycle of frescoes illustrates several episodes from the First Book of Samuel. Top left, God gives a warning to the Philistines by destroying the statue of their fish-god Dagon before striking Ashdod. The purpose was to convince the princes to return the Ark from their city to Beth-shemesh. Right, the first part of the Ark's journey through the Philistine cities that suffered new epidemics wherever the Ark of the Covenant went. In the end, to protect all who came into contact with the sacred object, the soothsayers decided that it should be placed on a cart drawn by two cows (bottom).

suffered by the people of Ashdod. Consequently, they hurried to direct the Ark to Ashkelon. There, as soon as they were seen from the lookout tower, the entire population broke out into yells of fear, and as the first deaths began to occur, they beseeched the princes to send the Ark back to the Jews. All well and good, but how might they avert the wrath of the Lord?

Called to consult on the matter, the Philistine priests and soothsayers decreed that they had to provide the Ark with five gold objects that symbolized the sickness that had struck them and five gold mice (the number five

and beseeched their fellow Jews in the nearby town of Kiriath-jearim to come and take the Ark away. It was taken to the house of the Levite Abinadab where it was entrusted to his son Eleazar who looked after it for twenty years.

Eli was succeeded as the religious leader of Israel by Samuel, who led the Jews to victory against the Philistines with the help of a violent storm that the Lord sent against the enemies of the Chosen People. The Philistines were so routed and humiliated that they did not dare to cross the borders between their lands and Israel.

Samuel was able to rule his people in peace, periodically gathering the representatives of the nation in his birthplace, Ramathaimsophim, called Ramah for short, where Deborah's palm tree grew. In the end, when Samuel was old, he passed some of his functions to his sons Joel and Abiah, but they "walked not in his ways, but turned aside after lucre, and took bribes, and perverted judgment" wrote the indignant Josephus. The people complained among themselves and, when they could take no more, they went to Ramah to tell Samuel, who was ignorant of his sons' dealings, and asked for a king to govern Israel. Reluctantly the prophet agreed and, with the help of God, chose a handsome, courageous and strong young man named Saul, who was a member of the tribe of Benjamin. Samuel anointed Saul in Ramah by pouring oil over his head, which was a solemn rite traditionally used in the Middle East and which can be seen in Egyptian tomb paintings. Then Samuel called the people to Mizpeh and presented them with their new king. Saul quickly won the favor of the people by leading them to victory against the Amonites. He was acclaimed king at Gilgal, near the twelve stones that Moses had taken from the Jordan. Saul chose the village of Gabaa as his residence. Gabaa means "peak" as the village stood on a hilltop a few miles north of the city of Jebus (later to become Jerusalem). The ruins of Gabaa have been excavated at Tell el-Ful (the "Hill of Broad Beans"). Saul's palace was modest; this was a simple people of shepherds and farmers. The throne room measured about 25 x 16 feet, and the double walls of the entire palace-fort measured no more than 135 x 200 feet. Even the pots and cups found in the ruins of the kitchen indicate a very simple life. If compared to the pharaohs of Egypt or even the rich and grand princes of Philistine, the first king of Israel was little more than a rustic crowned peasant but, as a warrior, he was a great general. Saul's son Jonathan, his first-born and due to succeed him, was likewise a great warrior. In various military campaigns Saul and he both repeatedly defeated the Amonites, Moabites, Edomites and Philistines. On the evening before the battle with one of these armies, however, Saul committed his first great sin; he was waiting impatiently for Samuel to bless the troops and make the propitiatory sacrifice to the Lord but the prophet was late. The soldiers began to worry and then to desert. To prevent the army melting away, the king decided to perform the rite himself. But Samuel, once he had arrived, harshly criticized the king and prophesied that Saul's sons would never reign, that his dynasty would end with himself.

Then the king committed his second error. He defeated the Amalekites but instead of killing them to the last man, woman and child, as the Lord had ordered him, Saul saved the lives of the prisoners, including their king Agag. In the name of the implacable God of

Israel, Samuel went to Saul and informed him that God had decreed he should be replaced as king, then the prophet cut Agag into pieces.

Having "repented that he had made Saul king over Israel," God ordered Samuel to go a village named Bethlehem in the land of Judah. There he indicated a young shepherd boy named David who would become the next king of Israel. Samuel anointed David as he had anointed Saul, then returned to Ramah. In his modest palace in Gabaa, Saul fell sick. It was a moral rather than physical sickness, a deep psychological prostration because God had sent an "evil spirit" to trouble him. His servants decided to send for a good harp player because music soothed the king's sufferings, so, as no one played the harp better than David, the shepherd boy was invited to court to console the king. David became a favorite of the king and was made his armor-bearer. Occasionally he returned to Bethlehem to graze his father's flocks.

In the meantime, the Israelites and Philistines waged incessant war. Their armies met at Socoh in the Valley of the Terebinth through which the River Elah runs. Today the Arabs call the valley Wadi es-Sant (Valley of Acacias). Here, for forty days, the two armies faced one another without coming to battle, and each morning and evening a Philistine soldier named Goliath, dressed in bronze and iron armor, went out of the Philistine ranks to challenge a champion of the Jews. Goliath stood six cubits and a span tall, that is, 12 feet 6 inches, so the Jews were too afraid to challenge him. He carried a spear that weighed 20 pounds as though it were a twig, and his servant went before him, almost crumpling under the weight of Goliath's shield. Saul's dismay was great and he searched for a champion to fight the giant, but to no avail despite offering gold and his daughter as a bride. But he was saved when David, the shepherd boy, presented himself before Saul and offered to fight Goliath. He told the king that he had killed a lion and a bear to defend his flock, and, with the help of God, that he would kill the Philistine. Struck by David's faith, the Jews dressed him in armor, but David, feeling too weighed down, removed the protection and took only his shepherd's staff and sling. Then he chose five smooth stones from the brook.

When David approached Goliath, the giant could not believe his eyes and he cursed him in the name of his gods and promised to give his "flesh unto the fowls of the air, and to the beasts of the field." But Goliath had not finished his ranting before a stone from David's sling struck him between the eyes and he fell to the ground. David ran to the body, unsheathed the immense sword and cut off the giant's head. Panic-stricken, the Philistines ran away, but were cut down by the Jews chasing after them.

146-147 David and Goliath *is a famous oil painting
(1606-07) by an artist at the height of his artistic skills:
Michelangelo Merisi, known as Caravaggio.
Characterized by an ambiguous sensuality typical of the
master's best works, the young and triumphant David,
his gaze defiantly forward and brandishing his short
double-edged sword in his right hand, holds the giant's
head by the hair.*

*147 The same scene of David and Goliath, painted more
theatrically by Titian in 1543 on the ceiling of the
sacristy of Santa Maria della Salute, Venice.*

Returning to the royal court, David became the close friend of Jonathan, the prince and heir to the throne, and he married Michal, Saul's younger daughter. However, the king's mind must have been disturbed because his behavior toward David was inconsistent: he admired him but feared him, he loved him but envied him the enormous popularity he had won among the people. On one occasion Saul wanted to kill David but backed down.

Faced by this contradictory treatment, David decided to flee for his life. He looked for refuge in Judah with 400 followers, and he sent his family to Moab to protect them from Saul's army. On two occasions the king found himself unknowingly at the mercy of David but the young man did not take advantage of the situation as he considered Saul his king and hoped simply that the man would return to sanity and cease hunting him unjustly.

So, when Saul spent the night in the same cave where David was hidden in the Judaean desert on the east bank of the Dead Sea, David cut off a piece of the king's skirt to show that he might have cut his throat. On another occasion, he slipped into the king's camp near Hebron and took the king's spear from his tent, again without harming Saul. All to no avail however as Saul refused to give in, and searched for David with greater hate than ever so that the young man was obliged to leave Israel and take refuge with the Philistines. Because of his reputation for courage and tactical skill, David was welcomed by King Achish, who assigned him the city of Ziklag for his residence. King Achish had to fight Saul in battle, and he wanted David to fight with him. It turned out that the Philistine soldiers did not trust David and thought he might turn and fight against them once the battle had started; in consequence, they convinced Achish to send David back to Ziklag. So neither David nor his small army participated in the battle of Mount Gilboa at which the Philistine archers cut down the Israelites in great number.

The defeat was overwhelming and Saul, who saw three of his sons killed, asked his armor-bearer to cut him down. This the man was unwilling to do, so Saul took his sword and fell upon it to avoid dying at the hands of the Philistines. He knew that he would die defeated as three days earlier he had visited a soothsayer in En-dor on the hills of Moreh and spoken to the spirit of the dead prophet Samuel. Samuel told the king that the Lord had deserted him and that he would lose the battle and his life.

Having decapitated the defeated Saul, the Philistines took his body and those of his sons and hung them up on the walls of Beth-shan, but during the night the bodies were taken away and buried by the inhabitants of Jabesh-gilead, who, many years previous, had been helped by Saul. David heard the news at Ziklag.

148 *The 17th century Neapolitan painter Salvator Rosa painted several works inspired by magic and witchcraft, including paintings of a religious nature. Here, the spirit of the dead Samuel (an old man wrapped in a cloak) is called upon by the soothsayer of Endor on behalf of Saul, who wanted to know the outcome of the battle of Mount Gilboa against the Philistines, during which, in fact, Saul and his sons were to be killed.*

148-149 *Pieter Bruegel the Elder, perhaps the most important Flemish painter of the 16th century, painted the Suicide of Saul in 1562. The depth and scope of the backdrop, the complexity of the action, and the dramatic nature of the events – all typical of Bruegel's best works – are fully appreciable in this oil painting. The Philistines overwhelm the Israelites as, on the rock to the left, the hapless king falls upon his sword.*

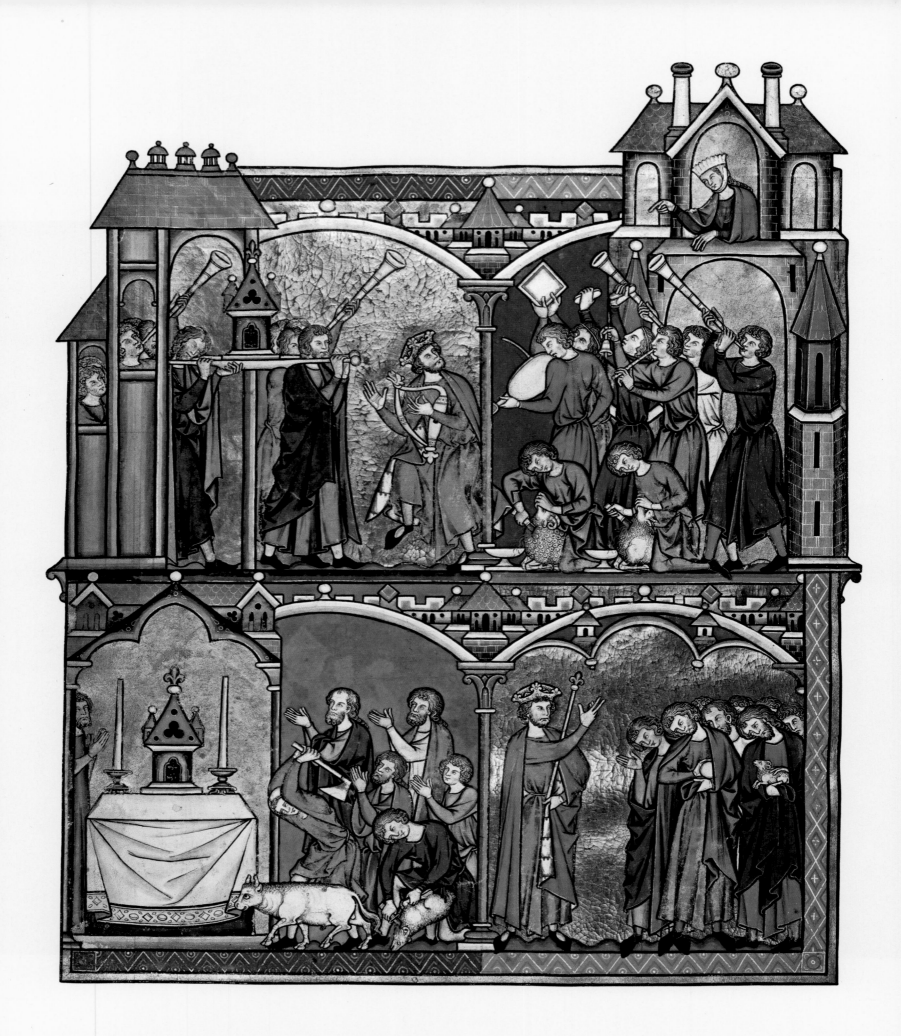

150 In the upper section of this illumination from the
Maciejowski Bible, David dances before the Ark of the
Covenant. He is watched from a palace window by his wife
Michal, who despises him for his unkingly behavior.
Bottom, the king celebrates a sacrifice when the Ark is
carried into the shrine and he blesses the people and
distributes food. Originally, the illuminations were the only
form of narration in this extraordinary work; the Latin text
was not added until the 14th century.

151 top This mosaic from St. Mark's, Venice, shows David
holding a cartouche in his right hand containing verse 11
of Psalm 131. According to the Roman antiphonary
(Psalterium Romanum), 'de fructu ventris tui ponam
super sedem meam' ('The fruit of your womb I will put on
my throne'); oddly, in the new version of the liturgical
psalter (the neo-Vulgate of 1979), the sentence ends 'your
throne'.

Israel no longer had a king and Saul's dynasty had ended as predicted by Samuel: the first king of Israel had paid for his sins. David mourned Saul and his son Jonathan, whom he had loved as a brother. He did not know what to do, so called for the Lord's help, who prompted him to go to Hebron. Here, at the cave of Machpelah, the sanctuary of the nation, he was elected king of the tribe of Judah at the age of thirty.

However, he was not recognized as king by the tribes of the north and they called on Ishbosheth, another of Saul's sons, to reign over them. Ishbosheth settled in the city of Mahanaim, which lay to the east of the Jordan, and went to fight David in battle. Civil war followed in which Ishbosheth continually came out the loser until he was killed seven years later by two of his own men in the hope they would be rewarded by David. When they came to him, however, David was horrified by the story and had the two killed for their treachery. This turn of events meant that Saul's line was now fully wiped out and the northern tribes came down to Hebron to proclaim David the sole king of Israel. He led his people to take Jebus – a key city because it controlled the highway that led to the east – which was occupied by the Canaanites, but they were convinced of its impregnability as it lay up on a rock and they sent David a message saying "Except thou take away the blind and lame, thou shalt not come in hither." Yet the Jews managed to enter the city and kill its defenders. David made it his capital as it was situated right in the center of the country on the border between Israel and Judah, and he

called it Jerusalem. There he built a palace with the help of carpenters, masons and cedar wood sent by his ally and friend, Hiram I, the Phoenician king from the coastal city Tyre. David "grew great, because the Lord God of hosts was with him," and wanted his residence to be the Holy City of the Chosen People. So he decided to move the Ark of the Covenant there, which till that day had remained in Kiriath-jearim. Thirty thousand delegates from across the kingdom accepted this proposal, and a majestic procession started out from the small village. The people followed behind the Ark, which had been placed on a new cart drawn by two oxen guided by Uzzah and Ahio, the two sons of the Levite Abinadab. David marched behind the cart, then came the crowd to the sound of harps, lutes, tambours, sistrums and cymbals. But when they came to Nachon, the oxen slipped on the ground and the Ark wobbled dangerously. Uzzah put out his hand to steady it but as soon as he touched it he was struck down dead by the Lord. Only the priests, according to the commandment of God, were allowed to place their hands on the sacred object. Mindful of the Lord's wrath, David ordered the Ark to be taken down there and then. Three months later, the journey restarted, this time accompanied only by priests, and the king who followed behind. To demonstrate humility, piousness and joy, David was dressed in a simple linen tunic like the priesthood, and he "danced before the Lord with all his might." Finally the Ark entered Jerusalem where it was placed in a new shrine on the hills of Zion.

151 bottom David plays the harp in an illumination taken from the Breviary belonging to King Martin I of Aragon (1395-1410). King Martin commissioned the work, which based on French breviaries, from the Cistercian monastery in Poblet, Catalonia, in about 1398.

David's wife, Michal, the daughter of Saul, watched as the procession arrived and saw from a palace window her husband dancing. She did not think it suitable and "despised him in her heart," The Lord, however, welcomed this homage and punished Michal by making her barren, which was a shameful codition for an Israelite woman.

David did have children, but by other wives and concubines. He loved women and had a harem like nearby kings, but to his shame, he was attracted to Bathsheba, the wife of an army officer named Uriah the Hittite. To have Bathsheba all to himself, he not only committed adultery with her, from which resulted a child, but ordered Uriah's commanding officer to send the man into the thickest part of a battle, where he would be left alone so that he might be killed. When this occurred, the Lord could not pardon such infamy and, through the spokesman Nathan the prophet, He condemned David who hastened to marry Bathsheba. God's anger was vented by causing the death of the baby, and only deep contrition on the part of the king prevented further disasters.

David's old age was marked by many dramas. His eldest son, Amnon, was guilty of evil when he raped his half-sister Tamar, and when the indulgent David did not punish him, it was Tamar's full-brother, Absalom, who took revenge by having Amnon killed two years after the event.

*152 **bottom*** *In this illumination (1500-25) by an anonymous artist, taken from a Book of Hours belonging to the Vasselin family, David falls in love with Bathsheba when he sees her bathing half naked in a pool.*

152-153 Scenes from the Bible Historiale: David in old age, now infirm and cloistered in his palace, and the choice of his successor, his son Solomon.

For a further three years, Absalom, David's favorite son, remained in exile with his maternal grandfather, the king of Geshur, which was a small Syrian kingdom in thrall to Israel; after that time, David pardoned his son and Absalom returned to the royal court. But Adsalom was impatient to rule in his father's stead as he considered the king an old, incapable man. When he and a group of followers started a revolt, forcing the king to leave Jerusalem and take shelter on the east side of the Jordan, the 60-year-old king raised an army and led it in search of Absalom. In the decisive battle, David's officers forced him to remain apart while Absalom escaped on horseback into the forest of Galaad. However, he rode under an oak tree whose branches hung down so low that Absalom got his head got caught between the boughs. The mule continued on, leaving Absalom hanging. Joab, David's most trusted general, then shot him through with three arrows.

Absalom's death was followed by new revolts and a terrible plague, and only at the last moment, following David's prayers, did the Angel of Death withdraw, leaving Jerusalem untouched by his lethal sword.

David's last years were spent in sadness and infirmity. He was practically an invalid and hardly left the palace. With the approach of the succession, his many sons hatched intrigues. When David died at the age of 70 (after reigning for 7 years over Judah and 33 years over all the Jews and various conquered lands) he had only recently chosen as his successor Solomon, his second child by his favorite wife, Bathsheba. This choice had been supported by the prophet Nathan. Solomon was to be the greatest of the kings of Israel and was destined to enter not just Israel's history, but legend.

153 *In another illustration from the* Bible Historiale, *the prophet Nathan scolds the king for marrying Bathsheba as he was already married to the sterile Michal. To show his anger, God kills the couple's firstborn but that is not enough to placate him: others among Bathsheba's children were to have unhappy fates, though Solomon was destined to rule over Israel with proverbial wisdom.*

THE SPLENDOR OF SOLOMON

154 *Around 1465 the artist Jean Fouquet illustrated the French manuscript of* Antiquities of the Jews *with twelve large illuminations. The French version was taken from the original of Flavius Josephus, the 1st-century Jewish historian. In this powerful depiction, Solomon's magnificent Temple in Jerusalem is interpreted as a Gothic cathedral in the form of a cube, probably an allusion to the stability of Solomon's reign.*

155 *The Judgment of Solomon as depicted in the English Windmill Psalter (circa 1270-90). This is the first known illustration of a windmill (hence the name of the Psalter). The windmill is lodged within the decorated initial letter at the top of the picture.*

INCIPIT PRLIPOVENON

In about 1000 BC, the young Solomon "succeeded his father David as king and was firmly established on the throne." He struck down all opposition, beginning with his half-brother Adonijah who, being the eldest of David's living sons, thought himself the legitimate heir to the throne. We do not know if Adonijah really plotted against Solomon or if the new king simply suspected him unjustly, but the fact remains that Solomon condemned Adonijah to death and the sentence was promptly carried out. This tactic of preventive repression was also used against the priest Abiathar, and General Joab for the death of Absalom; both had supported Adonijah's rebellion against his father David when the king had made the decision to leave the throne to Solomon. Protected by his priestly cloth, Abiathar was only exiled, but Joab died by the sword after being dragged from the tabernacle of the Ark where he had taken refuge.

Now Solomon was able to reign in peace. The first thing he did was to ensure he had an heir so he engaged in a political marriage the like of which Israel had never seen. His bride was the daughter of the pharaoh of Egypt and the match was like a revenge for the people who had lived in the Nile valley as slaves. The pharaoh, the region's most powerful ruler, welcomed the alliance was welcomed, and offered Gezer, the fortified city he had conquered from the Caananites, as a wedding present to Solomon.

While Jerusalem was being ringed with new walls, King Solomon went to Gibeon where the shrine with the altar of the sacrifices stood, and he made one thousand burnt offerings. The Lord appreciated this gesture and, the following night, he appeared in a dream to the king asking what gift he would like in return for his devotion. Solomon did not ask for honors or riches, but for a more precious gift: wisdom.

156-157 This priestly, static Byzantine image of Solomon is taken from the Souvigny Bible. Until 1793, this illuminated manuscript from the late 12th century belonged to the priorate of Souvigny, but then it passed into State ownership.

157 Solomon kneels in prayer before the shrine with the sacrificial altar. God appears and informs him that He will support him and his house. In the First Book of Kings (which tells the story of Solomon's life) the presence of God and His divine glory are symbolized by the cloud.

God agreed willingly to this request to the point that Solomon's wisdom to this day is proverbial. The king showed this wisdom a few days later when he made a judgment that has remained famous. Two "harlots" came before Solomon. Both given birth to a child at the same time on the same day, but one night, while they were all sleeping in the same bed, one of the two women had accidentally suffocated the other's baby with her weight. Now both claimed the surviving child, swearing that the baby that had died was the child of the other woman. There were no witnesses and no proof, simply the words of both women.

All the notables present at the scene were perplexed, incapable of deciding either way, but Solomon called one of his guards and ordered him to cut the baby in two so that each woman could have a half. At this inhuman sentence, one of the pair threw herself at the feet of the king and pleaded him to let the baby live so that the other woman could have it. The other woman, however, was prepared to let the sentence be carried out. This renunciation was a demonstration of true maternal love, concluded the king, and assigned the baby to the woman who was prepared to lose the infant so that he might be saved. The false claimant, however, was punished for her offence.

Being such a wise man, Solomon composed 3000 proverbs and 1005 songs, but most of these have been lost, like the books of botany and zoology he wrote. These books "discoursed of trees, from the cedar of Lebanon down to the marjoram that grows out of the wall, of beasts and birds, of reptiles and fishes." Josephus adds that God also gave Solomon knowledge of the art of magic, "which he used against demons to the advantage and relief of man. For this he wrote spells to cure sicknesses and left many forms of exorcism." His disciples were still practicing at the time that Josephus wrote, and he claimed to have seen a certain Eleazar free peo-

ple possessed by devils in the presence of Emperor Vespasian, his sons, and of all the Roman army during the siege of Jerusalem. Eleazar took a ring set with a root recommended by Solomon and held it in front of the nose of the possessed man. When the smell was changed, the devil was forced to come out of the man through his nostrils, and the man himself collapsed to the ground.

Eleazar chased the evil spirit away by pronouncing the spells of Solomon and, as further proof to the skeptics, he forced the invisible devil to tip over a water pot some distance away.

To the readers of *One Thousand and One Nights*, the extraordinary gifts of Solomon – known to the Arabs as Suleiman ben Daud – are familiar. He knew and spoke the language of all animals: those that walk, those that wriggle, those that fly and those that swim. He knew all things in heaven and on earth, evident and hidden; the angels obeyed him as they did the spirits, and, using the magic stones in his rings, he called them up and used them to suit his purposes. The winds transported him and all his troops on huge magic carpets; devils built him the most marvelous buildings. Further, anyone who opposed him was closed up in a bottle and thrown to the bottom of the sea or imprisoned in a jar from which some fisherman or Aladdin would liberate them, whether by good or bad fortune.

Josephus also informs us that Solomon "made silver as common in Jerusalem as stones." He was a rich king because he had successfully reorganized his kingdom by dividing it into twelve administrative districts whose boundaries deliberately did not coincide with those of the twelve tribes. He also created an efficient tax system that required duty to be paid by all caravans that crossed Palestine. He established a poll tax for all subject peoples and a tribute from each district, and he reserved to the state the monopolies on the sale of yarn, carts and horses.

158 In 1729 Giambattista Tiepolo began to fresco the ceiling of the 'Red Room' in the archbishop's palace in Udine. As it was used for the administration of ecclesiastical justice, Tiepolo decorated it with the Judgment of Solomon, one of the most symbolic episodes of the king's proverbial wisdom.

159 In the Raphael Rooms in the Vatican – named for the important frescoes the master painted there for Julius II and Leo X – the same episode is given strong, dramatic tones with the guard holding the baby in one hand and his sword in the other.

160 *This hypothetical reconstruction of the Temple of Solomon is from Nicolas de Lyre's 14th-century Bible. The building is more like a turreted castle than a temple as, during the Middle Ages, places and people were illustrated in contemporary style.*

He wanted to use all this money to realize his father David's dream, that of building a temple dedicated to the Lord who until then had never had one but had to be content with a mobile shrine such as the Ark of the Covenant. In his last years of life, David had accumulated large sums of money and stores of materials. He had also left his son the plan of the building, which had been inspired by God. Solomon prepared to start construction of the Temple by gathering all those raw materials that were still missing, and the workers who would bring it into being. These were provided by King Hiram of Tyre, who had been a close friend of David. Hiram's kingdom included the region of Lebanon where there grew gigantic cedars, whose highly quality wood, considered almost indestructible, was exported to

Egypt, Nineveh and Ecbatana, where it was used in important constructions. A formal agreement was drawn up in which, in return for payment in wheat, oil, wine and barley, the trees were cut and transported to the sea, then roped together to form large rafts and floated to the port of Jaffa. There, they were unroped and drawn by oxen for the twenty-five miles that separated Jerusalem from the Mediterranean.

The wood was accompanied by an expert Phoenician craftsman named Hiram (like the king of Tyre), whose father was Phoenician and mother Jewish. This Hiram was very skilled in all fields, said the Phoenician king in a letter to Solomon; he could work with "gold, silver, bronze, iron, stone and wood, cloth dyed blue and purple … and make all

kinds of sculpture and artistic objects." This extraordinarily capable man passed into legend as did his client, Solomon, and later became a sort of biblical patron of the Freemasons. An Islamic tradition says that Hiram was killed in the Temple by three of his assistants as soon as it was finished, owing to professional jealousy.

The Temple built by this architect is exalted in the Bible as a huge undertaking. In fact, compared to other monuments built during antiquity, it was rather modest in size. The Temple proper stood in the center of a huge four-sided enclosure and measured 124 feet long, 56 wide and 53 high -- only half the size of the Parthenon in Athens. However, it was very richly decorated: the Jews came from every part of the kingdom to admire it and, not knowing the immense buildings in Thebes (Egypt), Nineveh, or Babylon, they had no means of comparison and remained amazed as they passed beneath its 177 foot-high, gold-lined portico. The hand basins, branched candlesticks, candle-snuffers, thuribles and winged cherubim that guarded the Ark itself were all lined with gold, and some decorated with precious stones. The walls were made from square blocks of stone but the ceiling, doorposts and doors were of carved cedar and olive wood, and the floor was paved with cypress.

The sacrificial altar before the portico was 16 feet high and 33 feet long. Next to it stood a gigantic basin called the "Sea of Bronze," it stood on 12 bronze oxen and contained 200 gallons of water that was used by the priests in their purification ablutions.

Construction of the Temple took seven years and was completed by 120,000 men who worked in month-long shifts. When it was finished, the people and craftsmen dedicated a further thirteen years to the construction of an even larger house to be Solomon's palace, which would also contain the state's administrative offices, and the king's harem. This must have been very large as the Bible states that Solomon had 700 wives and 300 concubines, who would have required just as many slaves to serve them if not double that number. Consequently, it is easy to understand that the hall known as the "House of the Forest of Lebanon" – as it had columns made from cedar – was itself four times larger than the Temple.

ATRIVM SANCTVM

SANCTVM SANCTVM

ATRIVM

PROPHANVM

OCCIDENT

MERIDIES

ATRIVM GENTIVM

PROPHANVM

TEMPLI SALOMONIS ANTIQVI

SEPTENTRIO

162-163 The design of this spectacular 16th-century Flemish representation of the Temple in Jerusalem was the result of study of the Polyglot Bible edited by Benedictus Arias Montanus, a Spanish Orientalist, and published between 1568 and 1572.

163 A similar design, reproduced in an engraving of 1727, was the work of another famous biblical comentator, the Frenchman Auguste Calmet, who was active in the first half of the century.

166-167 Piero della Francesca painted a series of frescoes in the main chapel of the church of San Francesco in Arezzo, Italy, between 1452-66. The cycle is named the Story of the Cross and was inspired by a 15th-century text called the Legend of the Holy Cross. The episode shown – Solomon's meeting with the Queen of Sheba in Jerusalem – is part of the cycle.

167 bottom *Solomon and the Queen of Sheba are shown together in this elegant initial letter of an illuminated medieval manuscript. This is the letter 'O' which opens the second verse of the Song of Songs with the Latin words Osculatur me -- 'Let him kiss me with the kisses of his mouth!' (Song of Songs 1, 2)*

In this and other rooms decorated with statues, low-reliefs and frescoes, the king would give audience, exercise justice, and receive ambassadors and princes from other countries who visited to witness his wisdom and splendor. One of these visitors was the beautiful and magnificently attired Queen of Sheba. Sheba was the land that today is identified by some with the Yemen, by others with Ethiopia, but which in fact may have included both as they lie opposite one another at the southern tip of the Red Sea; the medieval kings of Christian Abyssinia claimed to be her descendants. She came, says Josephus, "with apparatus of great richness," followed by camels laden with gold, gems and spices. It was her intention to pose many difficult questions to Solomon, but he easily answered them and she recognized that his actual wisdom far exceeded the reports she had heard. When her curiosity was satisfied, she returned to Sheba.

Solomon did not ask the Phoenicians just for cedar and craftsmen as he wanted to turn Israel into a naval power as well. He had a small outlet onto the Red Sea with the two small ports of Ezion-geber and Elath, so his friend Hiram built him a bronze workshop there so that the metal extracted from the nearby mines of Edom could be processed. He also built a shipyard that produced a fleet to export the metal in the form of ingots, weapons, tools, nails and fishing hooks. Navigated by expert Phoenician sailors, the ships sailed right down the Red Sea, out through the strait of Bab el-Mandeb, and down the coasts of East Africa, India and the rich and mysterious country of Ophir, where the expedition loaded 400 gold talents, sandalwood, precious stones, silver and spices.

King Solomon was therefore surrounded by abundance; at the height of his glory, he sat on a throne of ivory and was surrounded by bodyguards who carried gold shields. But all this sumptuousness had made him forget the commandments of the Lord. He loved luxury and, in particular, women too much. He married many princesses from other nations and faiths and indulged their wishes to worship idols, allowing them to perform ceremonies in the City of David in honor of false gods. And so the God of Israel was angered and punishment was visited on his descendants.

THE DIVIDED
ᴋINGDOM

168 *In about 1452 Fra Angelico painted the panels that form the doors to the Silver Chest in the church of the Santissima Annunziata, Florence. The themes are both figurative and symbolic: the 'Mystical Wheel' is one of the latter and is an interpretation of Heaven according to the Book of Ezekiel. The outer wheel shows the prophets and the inner one evangelists and apostles.*

169 *This 13th-century manuscript from Mainz, Germany shows, from the top, the siege of Jerusalem, the Jews being led into exile in Babylon, and three of Jesus' forefathers cited in Matthew 1, 12-14 with their wives: Shealtiel, son of Jeconiah and father of Zerubbabel; Abiud, the son of Zerubbabel and father of Eliakim; and Azor, the son of Eliakim and father of Zadok.*

The new idols

Solomon died after reigning for 40 years, when he was perhaps 60 years of age. Despite his many wives and, therefore, a plethora of sons, he had no successor worthy of him. The heir to the throne was the 40-year-old Rehoboam, the son of an Ammonite princess, but he is described as a domineering fool. He gathered the representatives of the tribes in Shechem to proclaim him king but refused to compromise on the demands they made of him regarding the heavy taxation Solomon had imposed. A revolt broke out and the crowd stoned Adoram, the "commander of the forced levies," to death. Rehoboam fled to Jerusalem and the northern tribes chose instead Jeroboam to be their king. Jeroboam had returned from Egypt, where he had taken refuge from a death sentence Solomon had placed on him some years earlier. What had happened was that when the prophet Ahijah told Solomon that Jeroboam would reign over ten tribes of Israel, the king had ordered Jeroboam's death, but the young man fled to Egypt for safety.

Rehoboam reigned in Jerusalem over two tribes, those of Judah and Benjamin, which more or less represented the territory over which David had first ruled. The Egyptians profited from this division of the kingdom and some years later marched into Judah. They took the city of Jerusalem and removed large quantities of gold from the Temple and royal palace, including the gold shields that Solomon's guards carried. Naturally, the hand of God was behind this turnabout because the weak leader Rehoboam had allowed his wives – all foreign princesses – to worship idols. One of these wives, called Maanca, dared to build a temple dedicated to Ashrael in the royal palace.

But in the other half of the divided kingdom, Jeroboam was just as great a sinner: to halt and draw off the flow of pilgrims to the Holy City of Jerusalem, he had two other altars built, one in Bethel and the other in Dan, at the foot of Mount Hermon. On both of these he placed golden calf.

Horrified, the priests and true believers waited in the land of Judah while Jeroboam inaugurated the altar in Bethel with a magnificent ceremony. He was, however,

disturbed by the appearance of "a man of God," that is, a prophet, who announced long-term disasters and also an imminent upheaval. At these words, the altar split in two and the ashes of the sacrifice spread across the ground; the arm of the king – which was held outright as he ordered his guards to arrest the prophet – became as rigid as an iron bar. He was obliged to show extenuating contrition before the Lord restored its use to him. Under these two poor kings, both disgraced in the eyes of the Lord, Judah and Israel were perpetually at war with each other, and the conflict continued for almost fifty years under their successors, some of whom were

even more impious. Like Abijah of Judah, who "walked in all the sins of his father," and Baasha, who usurped the throne of Israel by assassinating Jeroboam's son. But Baasha's son, in turn, was killed by Zimri during a drinking session. Zimri took the throne but reigned only for one week before killing himself in a palace fire that he himself began when his rival, Omri, defeated him.

Inevitably, Omri "did what was wrong in the eyes of the Lord" and the Bible curtly condemns him. However, Omri must have been an exceptional personality as he succeeded in holding the Syrian kings in Damascus at bay and, much later, the Assyrians used to refer to Israel as "Mat Khamri," or "the land of Omri." He moved his capital to a hill in the center of a valley and he built a city there that he named Samaria. To strengthen Judah's traditional alliance with the Phoenicians, he married his son Ahab to the princess Jezebel, daughter of Ethbaal, the king of Sidon.

Ethbaal had taken the throne in Tyre by assassinating his predecessor. However, before becoming king, Ethbaal had been the high priest of Astarte, the goddess of fertility and pleasure, and his daughter had been raised in an atmosphere of fervid religious idolatry and herself become a devoted follower of Baal. Baal

was the supreme god of the Phoenicians, the "lord of the soil" who lived in the fields. He died each year at the end of the spring rains and rose again after the summer sun had dried out the ground, and he would soak the land once again with the autumn rains. When Ahab became king on the death of his father, he was persuaded by Jezebel to build a temple to Baal in Samaria and to dedicate a sacred wood to the god, as the Phoenicians did. Ahab also surrounded himself with priests of various divinities, while the queen persecuted the priests of the true God, even having some killed.

This blood-soaked royal couple was faced with the prophet Elijah, who was stern, ascetic, bearded and dressed only in a cloth wound around his loins. God sent rooks bearing food in their beaks to Elijah and gave him the strength to run at the same speed as Ahab's royal chariot. And he allowed Elijah to win the challenge the prophet had made to four hundred priests of Baal by sending down fire from Heaven to consume an ox Elijah had sacrificed on the altar while ignoring the rival sacrifice made by the priests of Baal. At this triumph and proof of the true God, the people of Israel rose up and slaughtered the representatives of Baal.

To escape Jezebel's vengeance, Elijah was obliged to take refuge in a cave in the Sinai, but the Lord enjoined him to return. During his journey back, Elijah met Elisha, whom he designated his successor. Following Ahab's death in battle against the Syrians (a death Micah had prophesied), Elijah challenged Ahab's son and successor Ahaziah, another "servant of Baal." The new king sent three contingents of fifty soldiers each to arrest the prophet but the first two were consumed by fire sent down from Heaven. The commander of the third behaved with respect towards the prophet and accompanied him to the palace in Samaria. There Elijah terrorized the king by announcing that his descendants would not reign because of the king's impiety.

When Elijah felt called by the Lord, he set off for the Jordan accompanied by Elisha and followed at a short distance by fifty more prophets who knew what was going to happen and wanted to be present. When they arrived at the river, Elijah struck the water with his cloak. The water then parted to let him and Elisha pass to the other bank. A chariot of fire drawn by horses of fire descended from Heaven and took Elijah up into the clouds. There, according to a later prophet, Malachi, Elisha would remain until he was sent back to Earth to perform another mission – "at the time of the second coming of Jesus Christ," according to some commentators.

172 In the Casa Ricciarelli in Siena, Daniele da Volterra (called 'il Braghettone' for having painted loin cloths over Michelangelo's nudes in the Sistine Chapel in 1564) painted a tired and ragged Elijah among dark shadows in net contrast to the serene and tranquil landscape behind him.

172-173 *In this 17th-century painting, Johann Heinrich Schoenfeld portrayed the first prophet of Israel as he inveighed against the followers of Baal, calling upon the Jews to worship the one, true God. It is no coincidence that the Hebrew version of his name, Eliyyah, means 'God is Yahweh.*

174 This 18th-century Bulgarian icon shows scenes from
the life of Elijah. Center, the prophet is fed by ravens in an
event that symbolizes the will of God that also governs
nature: '… and I have commanded the ravens to feed thee
there' (I Kings 17, 4).

175 The ascension (or better, the 'abduction') of Elijah to Heaven is illustrated with bright colors in this Greek icon from the late 17th century. Elisha, the successor to the great prophet Elijah, is shown beneath a chariot drawn by four flaming horses.

Elisha picked up Elijah's cloak and struck the waters again to return without wetting his feet, and he was fêted as Elijah's heir by the fifty prophets waiting on the west bank. A few years later Jezebel got her comeuppance. While she was looking out of a window in the royal palace hurling insults at Jehu, the commander of the army, accusing him of the death of her son Joram, she was flung out by the palace eunuchs and trampled by Jehu's horse. Her body was then devoured by dogs as Elisha had predicted. Elisha performed many miracles, the most remarkable of which was the liberation of Samaria, the capital of Israel, from the armies under Ben-hadad, the king of Syria, who was besieging the city. Samaria had seemed to be at the end of its resistance as the inhabitants were desperate from hunger when, invoking the Lord, Elisha conjured up a din of galloping horses, chariots and trumpets behind the Syrian troops at night. Thinking themselves attacked by the Hittites, the besiegers retreated toward Damascus in confusion. When peace had returned, Ben-hadad, who was gravely ill, sent his messenger Hazael to Elisha to ask him what his fate would be: would he live or would he die? The prophet replied that the king would die but not as a result of his sickness, and that it would be Hazael who would replace him on the throne. Hurrying back to Damascus, Hazael fulfilled the prophecy by suffocating Ben-hadad with a heavy cloth soaked in water

and proclaiming himself king of Syria. He then restarted the war, conquering that part of Israel to the east of the Jordan and attacking Judah. To save itself, the city of Jerusalem was obliged to hand over the Temple treasure; so, where the capital of Israel had suffered cruelly, the capital of Judah too was in trouble. Both kingdoms were ruled by men who had attained their position through bloodshed. For a few years an energetic and self-willed woman unified the two crowns. This was Athaliah, the daughter of Ahab and Jezebel, who was as wicked as both her parents had been. She married Joram, king of Judah, but on his death her son Ahaziah took the throne. As a descendant of Ahab, Ahaziah claimed rights to the crown of Israel that had been usurped by Jehu, but Jehu removed this threat by having Ahaziah killed. At this point, Athaliah decided to reign herself and set out to have all the children of Ahaziah killed, in other words, her own grandchildren. Thanks to the action of a nurse, a young boy named Joash survived, and was brought up in secret. Six years later, he was crowned king and the evil Ahaziah was assassinated by a group of conspirators. The only survivor of David's line, Joash reigned for forty years. His son Amaziah had a shorter but tormented reign and, in the end, was forced to flee Jerusalem to escape a plot to kill him. His flight was useless however as his enemies caught up with him and put him to death.

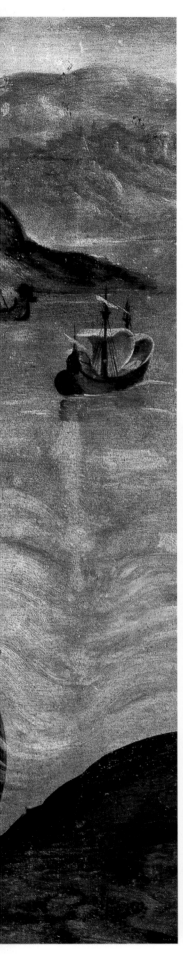

178 *In 1606, an anonymous artist painted the episode in which the prophet Jonah (8th century BC) was thrown into the sea by the crew of a ship on which he had fled trying to avoid God's instructions to preach in the city of Nineveh.*

179 *The prophets Isaiah, Hosea and Micah – shown here in the mosaics in St. Mark's, Venice – played a central role in the history of the Chosen People: called to interpret the signs of the times in every field (social, political and religious), they denounced every deviation from God's way.*

At the start of the 8th century BC, better times came with two kings who were worthier than their predecessors. These were Jeroboam II in Israel and Oziah in Judah. The first defeated the Syrians and conquered the kingdom of Damascus, while the second conquered the Philistine cities on the coast. It was a period of great economic prosperity as is shown by the jewelry and other luxury items found in the excavations of Samaria, and by the accounting tablets, which describe an opulent court.

The conquered peoples paid tributes, and trade, agriculture and livestock flourished. As usual, the only people to be unhappy were the prophets, who never ceased inveighing against sins of all kinds and continually prophesied disaster. One was Jonah, whom God had ordered to preach in the iniquitous city of Nineveh, but he disobeyed and fled to sea, only to be thrown overboard by the crew and swallowed by a whale. He was ejected onto terra firma three days later and immediately hurried to Nineveh, understanding that he could not disobey God.

Another was Amos who preached enraged sermons near the altars of the Golden Calf, lambasted the courtiers in Samaria and called their wives "cows." The more refined Hosea railed against the corruption of the people's customs, Micah saw "the threat of blood" everywhere, and sons in revolt against their fathers and daughters against their mothers. He predicted the downfall of Samaria and an even more ruinous fate for Jerusalem, which would be abandoned, reduced to a pile of rubble and plowed up like a field. Isaiah repeated Micah's prophesies but also saw further ahead and predicted that, after the suffering, there would be a gentle future in which "swords will be used as plowshares" and nations will no longer arm themselves against one another.

180 A great man of moral strength and wisdom, the
prophet Micah is portrayed on the back of the doors of the
polyptych of the Mystical Lamb, a masterpiece of Flemish
painting. Begun by Hubert van Eyck, it was completed in
1432 by his brother Jan.

181 Almost a century later, in 1512, Michelangelo painted
the human face of Isaiah on the Sistine Chapel ceiling. We
see the prophet with a hand to keep his place in the pages
of a book as he turns to two putti who are attracting his
attention. The seven prophets portrayed in the Sistine
Chapel represent either the wait for the advent of the
Savior and the hope of His coming, or the seven gifts
of the Holy Spirit.

The Assyrian threat

As usual, the pessimists were right. With the death of Jeroboam II, the crimes and conspiracies began once more, and while Israel was reeling from wars of succession, from the north arrived a new threat. These were the Assyrians under the king that the Bible refers to as Pul and historians as Tiglath-pileser III, who invaded the small kingdom with an immense army. Samaria was only able to save itself by paying the huge tribute of one thousand silver talents, but this was only a taster as the Assyrians returned several times and, in 727 BC, Samaria was once more besieged. After three years it surrendered and was forced to pay much more heavily. An inscription archaeologists found in the palace of the Assyrian king Sargon II in Dur Sharrukin (today Khorsabad) on the Tigris, north of Nineveh, says, "in the first year of my reign I besieged Samaria and conquered it. I took 27,290 prisoners alive and I took 50 splendid silver chariots for my royal armaments." The Samaritans were deported to Assyria and Midia and their place taken by Syrians. This event marked the end of the kingdom of Israel and its ten tribes, which now became the Lost Tribes. They disappeared into the darkness of history but have regularly been resuscitated by legend, and were even claimed by some eccentric researchers to be the indigenous peoples of the Americas.

The king in Jerusalem during that period was Hezekiah, who was dear to the Lord for his devotion, and so God healed the king from a serious illness that had taken him almost to death's door. The small kingdom of Judah had of course had to give way to the power of Assyria and pay a heavy tribute. But the yoke of the Assyrians was insupportable not just to the Jews: all the vassal states in the vast Assyrian Empire tried to shake off their chains. With the pretext of congratulating Hezekiah for his recovery, an ambassador arrived in Jerusalem from Merodach-Baladan, the king of Babylon. In fact his real purpose was to propose an anti-Assyrian alliance with Judah, Egypt, Edom, Moab, Phoenicia and the Philistines. Hezekiah accepted, and to ingratiate himself even more with the ambassadors, he showed them his treasure. This action outraged the prophet Isaiah, who warned the unwary king that not only all his wealth but the entire people of Jerusalem would one day be deported to Babylon.

Meanwhile the Assyrians had got wind of what was going on and their irresistible army, led by Sennacherib, came down to put out any pretence at rebellion. Seeing that he was incapable of withstanding so many troops, Hezekiah confessed to having conspired against the Assyrians, asked for pardon and offered to pay such a heavy sum that it was necessary to remove the gold linings on the Temple doors.

But this offer was not enough and Sennacherib had decided to punish Jerusalem by marching on the city. However, before he could attack the city, he was obliged to face down the Egyptians, and when he had routed them, before he could turn against Hezekiah, his army was struck down by an epidemic that, according to the Bible, killed 185,000 of his men in a single night.

Once Sennacherib's army had returned to its own country, Judah was able to enjoy a few years of peace. But the good king Hezekiah was succeeded by his wicked son Manasseh, who rebuilt the altars to Baal that his father had knocked down, and, in consequence, suffered another Assyrian invasion, one which ended with Manasseh being imprisoned in babylon. The king regretted his stupidity and asked God for pardon. God then returned Manasseh to his throne, where he remained for forty-five years, longer than any other king of Judah.

182-183 The vicissitudes of Hezekiah, king in Jerusalem during the life of Isaiah, were so dense with meanings regarding faith and divine reward that it inspired many artists in the 17th century. In the dramatic Defeat of Sennacherib, *painted circa 1615, Peter Paul Rubens depicts the defeat of the Assyrian armies by God in a wave of bodies, events and emotions.*

The fall of Jerusalem

When Manasseh's son Amon came to the throne, he once again returned to the forbidden idolatry and was killed by his own servants after just two years on the throne. His son, Josiah, was still a child but conformed to the commandments handed down by God. Josiah persecuted the worshippers of false gods, thereby winning the admiration of the prophet Jeremiah. Josiah was 39 years old and had reigned for 31 years when he was obliged to fight the Egyptian army under Pharaoh Necho II, who was marching north to unite with the Assyrians against the Babylonians. During the battle on the plain of Megiddo, an arrow struck him from which he later died. Shortly after, the Babylonians defeated the Assyrian Empire and divided the spoils with the Midians. Syria and Palestine were given to Nebuchadnezzar, the king of Babylon, who toured his new possessions to confirm his authority and to demand payment of tribute.

In Jerusalem, the new overlord deposed Jehoiakin (Josiah's son) and exiled him and his court to Babylon. In his place, Nebuchadnezzar installed Jehoaikin's uncle, Mattaniah, who changed his name to Zedekiah. Despite warnings from the prophet Jeremiah, the young Zedekiah committed at least two mistakes: "he did what was wrong in the eyes of the Lord" and he

rebelled against the Babylonians. So, in the ninth year of Zedekiah's reign Nebuchadnezzar's army besieged Jerusalem. Two years passed during which time all attempts at assault on the city failed, but hunger reduced the city to desperation. In 587, Just as Jerusalem was about to surrender, Zedekiah tried to flee at night by climbing over the city walls with his family, courtiers and a body of guards and heading for the Jordan valley. The Babylonians, however, were vigilant and gave chase.

Abandoned by his guard, the king was captured on the plain of Jericho, and taken to Riblah near Damascus before Nebuchadnezzar. One by one Zedekiah's sons were killed before his eyes, then his eyes were put out. To end his life, Zedekiah was taken in chains to Babylon and thrown into a dungeon where he remained till his death. His capital was put to an equally horrible end. The Temple, palace and buildings were stripped of all things of value and burned to the ground, and the walls of the city were knocked down. For the following half century, the Holy City, the City of David and of Solomon, was no more than a pile of rubble: all the inhabitants had been taken away in captivity to Babylon.

184 bottom and 184-185
The Bibliothèque de l'Arsenal in Paris has an illuminated manuscript produced in France around 1410 that may have belonged to Jean sans Peur, duke of Burgundy. It illustrates the Decameron *by Boccaccio. Here we see the destruction of the Temple in Jerusalem and the deportation of the Jews to Babylon.*

185 bottom *The Jews are led in chains before the Babylonian king Nebuchadnezzar (6th century BC) in this illumination from St. Elizabeth's Psalter. The highly refined work was produced by four or more artists in the Thuringian-Saxon school between 1200 and 1217 and was perhaps offered as a present at the wedding between Sophia of Saxony and Hermann, the landgrave of Thuringia.*

FROM THE
𝕭ABYLONIAN CAPTIVITY
TO THE MACCABEAN REVOLT

186 *Josephus, an officer in the Jewish army, was taken prisoner by the Romans in 70 AD and became a historian of the empire. In his work* Antiquities of the Jews *(the history of the Jewish world up to the war of AD 66), he narrates the taking of Jerusalem by the Seleucid king Antiochus IV Epiphanes, who sacked and profaned the Temple. The scene is portrayed in a 15th-century manuscript that illustrates Josephus' work.*

187 *In this coeval French illumination, the army of Cyrus of Persia captures Babylon in 539 BC, leading to the Jews being allowed to return to Israel. Some 50,000 were brave enough to leave an established economy, risk the dangers of a long journey to Jerusalem and an uncertain future. On their return to the Promised Land, they rebuilt Jerusalem and the Temple.*

By the waters of Babylon

he procession of exiles reached Babylon after a long and painful march. The appearance of the city and its surroundings certainly made an impression on them. It was not a pile of back-to-back huts hanging over narrow, twisting lanes or perched on the sides of steep hills like Jerusalem. It was a vast metropolis that stretched out of view into the plain on either side of a river. It had massive defensive walls and a grid of streets laid out orthogonally. The widest, the Processional Way, started from the polychrome Ishtar Gate and ran past the Hanging Gardens. The gate was decorated with enameled brick low reliefs and the gardens were later to be considered one of the Seven Wonders of the World. Opposite, there stood the Temple of Ninmach (the Great Mother and goddess of the Afterworld) that looked like a fort with its white plastered walls and many towers. Further up the Processional Way was the Etemenaki, the seven-storey ziggurat that stood 295 feet high above a square plinth that itself was 295 feet long on each side. The steps to climb the ziggurat were external and, as Herodotus tells us with a certain note of relief after climbing it in 460 BC, "halfway up there is a platform with seats to rest on." On the last platform there rose a large temple with a gold table and gold bed richly covered. Here, each night, the god Bel-Marduk came down from heaven to sleep, and was welcomed by a priestess. No other human could remain up there from sunset to dawn.

The city had more than fifty other temples and

teemed with people: long-haired men who wore perfumed linen tunics, woolen cloaks, and miters on their heads. Each one had a cylindrical seal around his neck and carried a carved staff. The sacred prostitutes who practiced their profession in the enclosure of the Temple of Militta (the Babylonian Venus) offered themselves to visitors to the city. It was a religious duty that had to be performed at least once, and the richly attired women fulfilled it on their luxurious covered carriages surrounded by a large retinue of slaves.

The busiest sections of the city were the embankments along the Euphrates. A bridge rested on eight pylons and was high enough for both small and large boats to pass beneath. The round frames of the boats were made from willow-tree branches covered with skins and lined with straw. Maneuvered by poles, these round boats were carried by the current down from the Assyrian mountains, bringing all kinds of goods with them, for example, goatskins of wine and even livestock. There was always at least a donkey on board because, once the boatmen had sold their cargo and the wooden frame and straw, they rolled up the animal skins, loaded them on the donkey and returned to the mountains on foot with the profits of the trip.

The sick used to lie in public along the river bank where travelers and country-dwellers going to the city to buy or sell wares would pass, as it was the custom for each passer-by to give advice to the sufferers on which cure to follow to get better.

188 bottom and 189 bottom During the reign of Nebuchadnezzar, the Processional Way and Ishtar Gate in Babylon were decorated with processional lions and mushkhush *(dragons of the god Marduk).*

188-189 This reconstruction of the royal palace in Babylon was the work of Johann Bernhard Fischer von Erlach in 1721 to illustrate his Entwurf einer historischen Architektur *(Outline for a Historical Architecture).*

SPECTACVLA BABYLONICA.

190 and 191 Vasily Surikov was a 19th-century master of
historical scenes. In Belshazzar's Feast *he illustrates the
episode narrated in Daniel 5, 1: 'King Belshazzar gave a
great banquet for a thousand of his nobles and drank wine
with them.' Then mysterious words were written on the wall
that only Daniel – shown as a young man in the Sistine
Chapel (right) – could interpret. He made a prophecy that
came to pass during the night with the death of the king.*

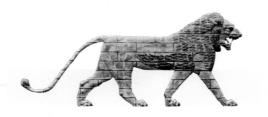

This magnificent imperial capital was surrounded by vegetable gardens, orchards, flower gardens, and groves of date palms and pomegranate trees. Here the captive Jerusalemites must have suffered from nostalgia, but not physically. Once settled in the city and its immediate surroundings, they were not considered slaves but inhabitants obliged to provide forced labor – which consisted mainly of digging and maintaining the irrigation canals that were essential to the region's economy. Otherwise they were just like all the other peoples in the empire, Babylonians included, and were able to practice their own livelihood. They could do any type of work. Some Jews cultivated the fields and raised livestock, but many discovered that in that huge city they had a vocation for trading. Many got rich and the poorest were provided with food on a daily basis from royal stores. In fact, the Jewish colony in Babylon was one of the wealthiest and largest of the diaspora that continued until the middle of the next century.

The exile of the Jews in a foreign land, as almost always happens, strengthened their sense of racial identity and, in consequence, their religious devotion. This was stimulated at first by sermons the prophet Ezekiel preached; he comforted the faithful by telling them that their 'Babylonian captivity' would not last longer than seventy years. The Jews were free to observe their own religion provided that they respected the religions of others in that land of many gods. Not having the Temple of Jerusalem any more they gathered for prayers and religious instruction in "assemblies," called synagogues in Hebrew.

Finally the seventy years of exile set by the Lord as a punishment for the recalcitrant Chosen People came to an end, as indeed the Babylonian Empire also did. To the east a new power arose and, in 539 BC, the army of Cyrus of Persia besieged the walls of Babylon. From the top of the towers the inhabitants watched amazed as the Persians undertook a task that was as exhausting as it was incomprehensible: the digging of a deep dike around the city. The Babylonians thought that the Persians wanted to isolate the city and prevent food or help from entering, but this did not worry them too much as they had enough food for years in the stores. However, Cyrus' plan was to deviate the waters of the Euphrates so that his army could enter the city along the resultant dry river bed.

When this occurred one night, taken by surprise, Babylon was taken in a trice. That evening, while its last king, Belshazzar, was banqueting in the palace, God came to foretell the dreadful downfall of the king, city and empire. A hand appeared out of thin air and wrote the mysterious words "Mene Mene, Tekel, U-pharsin" on the wall, which was Aramaic for "weighted, counted, divided." None of the Babylonian wise men was able to explain the meaning even though their fame had circled the world. Then, on the advice of the king's grandmother, a Jew was called. This was Daniel, who had "the gift of interpreting dreams, explaining riddles and unbinding spells," the same Daniel who was to finish up in the lions' den in Persia. It was he who explained to the astonished Belshezzar that God had weighed him in the balance and found him wanting, and that in consequence his kingdom was to be divided between the Medians and the Persians. And just a few hours later Babylon's destiny was fulfilled.

192 *After Babylon fell in 516 BC, Cyrus of Persia rebuilt the Temple in Jerusalem. This is narrated in the Book of Ezra (Esdras), which begins with the king's edict. Esdras led one of the first group of returning Jews, who had to face the hostility of those who had settled in Israel while the Jews had been held in slavery in Babylon. The reconstruction of the Jewish Temple is illustrated in Guiard des Moulins'* Bible Historiale, *in the copy held in the Russian National Library, St. Petersburg.*

There were no massacres, deportations, destruction of temples or sacking. The forbearing Cyrus only wanted his new subjects to recognize that he was now their ruler; apart from that they could continue with their normal lives. Moreover, he allowed the peoples that had been deported by the Babylonians to return to their own land if they so wished. Many Jews took advantage of this offer but not all; perhaps not even the majority as the Bible gives the figure of fifty thousand. All those who had created a position for themselves – craftsmen, merchants, money-changers and those that might be called bankers – preferred the prosperity that they had created for themselves to an uncertain future in a land they had never known.

One group departed immediately for Jerusalem guided by a prince of the kingdom of Judah called Sheshbazzar, whom Cyrus appointed governor of Jerusalem. The Jews had a difficult journey home, but after their arrival the autumn rains of 538 BC began, indicating it was the right season for plowing and sowing to provide a harvest the following year. On Mount Zion the Jews built a temporary altar that would serve them until the Temple was rebuilt. This had to wait many years and was only carried out during the reign of the new king of Persia, Darius. In this period the second wave of Jewish immigrants arrived in Judah from Babylon, under the command of Zerubbabel, a descendant of David, and Joshua, the grandson of the last high priest, with the moral support of the prophets Haggai and Zechariah. Built on its original site, the second Temple was larger than the first but did not have the same majesty or richness of decoration. When it was completed, in 515 BC, the elderly Jews that remembered Solomon's temple were disappointed and many wept. Separated from the city by a stone wall, the new Temple, like the previous one, had an external court with stores and accommodation for the priests along the wall. There was also an internal court closed off by a wall, in the center of which stood the sacrificial altar. The sanctuary was empty: the Ark of the Covenant had disappeared during the sacking of the city by the Babylonians all those years earlier. Nor was there any longer a political center to the Jewish state. Solomon's great palace had been reduced to ashes and could not be rebuilt as Jerusalem had no king, simply a governor appointed by a foreign ruler.

193 top *Gustave Doré illustrated this scene of the rebuilding of the Temple for the famous Bible published in France in 1865. He depicted hundreds of biblical scenes in an attractive and influential style that even affected the nascent cinema.*

193 bottom *An unusually magnanimous ruler for the period, Cyrus gave the Jews their freedom. This rational depiction of the episode is taken from a 19th-century book that reproduces several paintings by the 15th-century Frenchman, Jean Fouquet.*

194-195 *Queen Esther is a fondly regarded figure in Jewish history. Here she receives the crown from the hands of Asahuerus in a late 15th-century painting by the Florentine Jacopo del Sellaio, a pupil of Fra Filippo Lippi.*

195 *In the airy interior taken from a panel on a painted chest, Filippino Lippi (son of Filippo Lippi) – whose libertine behavior resulted in 1461 in his having to renounce his vows – illustrates three moments from the life of Esther: left, Mardochaeus laments the unhappy destiny of the Jews; center, Esther faints before the king; and right, Haman in vain requests pardon.*

The governors of the Persian Empire always treated their Jewish subjects benevolently. The favorite wife of one of them, Artaxerxes I, was a Jew named Hadassah, the adopted daughter of Mardochaeus, who foiled a plot ordered by the wicked prime minister Haman whose plan it was to exterminate the Jews. Haman had had a gallows built to hang Mardocheus but it was Haman himself who was hanged and Mardochaeus who took his place. The Jewish names of the characters in this story are Esther (Hadassah) and Ahasuerus (Artaxerxes), who are remembered even today by the Jews at the time of the festival of the Purim, which falls in February or March and ends with festivities.

196 The prophet Esdras was a scribe and legislator who refounded worship in Jerusalem. He was portrayed in the 1490s by the Castilian painter Pedro Berruguete on the predella panel of the ex-voto painting in the church of Santa Eulalia in Paredes de Nava, the painter's place of birth.

197 The upper register of this illumination is taken from a codex of the Romance d'Alexandre *produced in Flanders between 1338 and 1344. It illustrates the arrival of the Macedonian conqueror in Jerusalem. Center and bottom, one of Darius' envoys and a bearded man appear before the king of Persia.*

Xerxes successor, Artaterxes I, sent Esdras (a priest in the Jewish community that had remained in Babylon) back to Jerusalem with 1,700 Jews. Esdras imposed the observance of Mosaic Law and dissolved the many marriages that had taken place between Jews and non-Jews in the meantime. Some years later, another morally upright Jew, Nehemiah, who was the royal cupbearer at the Persian court (a position that required great trust by the king when poisoning was such a common occurrence) was saddened by the stories of the desolation of Jerusalem. He asked Artaxerxes permission to go to Judah and rebuild the city walls. The king not only agreed but appointed Nehemiah the governor of Judah and gave him a large escort. With the help of the people, and despite the hostility of neighboring Arab and Ammonite tribes, the walls of Jerusalem were rebuilt in just fifty-two days, as the Bible claims triumphantly. However, the more realistic Josephus claims that the actual period was two years and four months.

A century later, the Persian Empire fell to a conqueror from Macedonia: Alexander the Great. Having reached Syria, he headed south to invade Egypt, which was then a Persian satrapy. On his way to Egypt he first took Tyre, then Gaza, then prepared to march on Jerusalem to punish the city that had declared itself faithful to Darius, king of Persia. However, as the eloquent Josephus wrote, when his army came in sight of the city and the soldiers were anticipating massacre and looting, the people came out from the walls of the city wearing white tunics "with in front the priests wearing fine linen and the pontiff in a hyacinth robe embroidered with gold, wearing a miter on his head and above that a gold plate engraved with the name of God." Next, to the amazement of the Greek army, who believed Alexander out of his mind, the Macedonian knelt in front of the high priest. To his friend Parmenio, he explained that he was not honoring the man but the God the priest represented as the Lord had appeared to him in a dream when he was still in Macedonia and blessed his plan of conquering Asia.

Then Alexander made a sacrifice in the Temple in accordance with the dictates of the Hebrew liturgy explained to him by Jadduah. On the following day, Alexander allowed Jews living not just in Judah, but all the Persian Empire that he still had to conquer, the freedom to live in accordance with Mosaic law and to be exempt from the payment of tributes every seventh year. Grateful and enthusiastic, many young Jews enrolled in his army and followed him on the march to conquer Egypt, then Persia.

On Alexander's death eight years later, the immense territory he had conquered – from the Adriatic to the Indus, and from Armenia to Cyrenaica – was carved up among his generals. Palestine was disputed between the Ptolemies of Egypt and the Seleucids of Syria. These were tumultuous years, and many Jews decided to emigrate from Judah to settle either in Cyrene or in the new Egyptian capital, Alexandria, founded by the Macedonian general. This city soon became the richest and most cultured in the ancient world, and boasted the famous library built for Ptolemy II Philadelphus. Anxious to collect all the books that existed, this learned king ingratiated himself with Eleazar – the high priest in the Temple of Jerusalem – by sending gifts and liberating 120,000 Jews who had been enslaved in Egypt by his predecessor Ptolemy I Soter. He then asked him to send the Bible with some wise men who could translate it from Hebrew into Greek. Eleazar sent 72 translators to Alexandria and they completed the work on the island of Pharos (so they would not be disturbed by the noise of the city) in the 72 days schedued by Ptolemy. The translators were given separate rooms and were unable to consult one another but, even so, at the end of the set period their translations matched perfectly because, it is said, behind them there was the hand of God at work.

The pharaoh of Egypt fifty years later, Ptolemy IV Philopator (222-205 BC), had perhaps assassinated his father to win the crown, but definitely his mother and younger brother. This king went to Palestine to confront Antiochus III, the king of Syria, who intended to take the country. Having defeated the Syrians, Ptolemy went to Jerusalem where he wished at all costs to enter the Temple to celebrate his victory with a sacrifice, but he was met with the indignant protests of the high priest and the public. As soon as he set foot in the Temple, he experienced holy terror and his bodyguards were obliged to carry him out senseless. To obtain revenge, after returning to Alexandria, he attempted to force the Jews of the city to worship the Egyptian gods by threatening to have them trampled by war elephants if they refused. In the event, the elephants turned on the Egyptian soldiers and crushed them instead.

After the death of Ptolemy IV in 203 BC, Antiochus III of Syria took advantage of the power vacuum to invade Palestine once again and this time he succeeded in occupying it, but he was later defeated by the Romans. His son, Seleucus IV, who was obliged to pay the new conquerors war tribute, decided to ransack the Temple where he had been told there was an incalculably valuable treasure. He sent his chief minister, Heliodorus, to Jerusalem to confiscate it but on his arrival the priests prostrated themselves at the Altar of the Holocausts and the inhabitants ran into the streets wailing with their arms in the air. Unmoved, Heliodorus entered the Temple with a platoon of soldiers but there appeared before them a horse mounted by a dreadful rider. Heliodorus was knocked down by the horse's front legs while two angels whipped him until he lay down "wrapped in darkness." He was carried out on a stretcher and the high priest had to ask the Lord to return Heliodorus to life, then he consented to the urgent pleas of the Syrian soldiers who wished to leave Jerusalem immediately.

198-199 In the Expulsion of Heliodorus, *a fresco painted by Eugène Delacroix in 1861 in the chapel of the Santi Angeli in the church of Saint-Sulpice in Paris shortly before his death, a mysterious knight breaks into the Temple to punish the Syrian prime minister and prevent him from confiscating the treasure. The power of the drawing lies in its skilful use of vibrant colors, bringing life to what might be considered the master's artistic testament.*

200 *Antiochus IV Epiphanes is shown besieging Jerusalem, which has been transformed here into a powerfully fortified medieval city. The picture is taken from the* Chronique Universelle *(1480-82) and is known as the 'Bouquechardière' after its author, Jean de Courcy, lord of Bourg-Achard in Normandy.*

Relations with the Syrian dynasty worsened further when Antiochus Epiphanes had his brother Seleucus killed and took his place. The new king came to Jerusalem with a large army. He stripped the Temple bare of all valuables, including the curtains, erected a statue to Zeus, had pigs sacrificed, burned the sacred books, destroyed part of the walls, built a fort in which he maintained a Syrian garrison and prohibited the Jewish faith, repose on the Sabbath, and circumcision. Anyone who disobeyed was put to death. Mothers who had their sons circumcised were led through the city and then pushed off the city walls with their children. This was the first religious persecution in history. Jerusalem even lost its name and was called Antioch in Judah.

The oppression was so heavy that it naturally brought reactions. All across Judah the discontent rose to levels of fury. The first gesture of revolt came from a priest named Mattathias who lived in the village of Modein not far from Jerusalem. As occurred in all the large and small communities of the country, a Syrian soldier came to him to impose the worship of idols on the Jews. Mattathias not only refused but, when the soldier prepared to make a sacrifice to Zeus, he killed him. Mattathias then tried to flee with his family, the Has-

moneans, to the caves in the surrounding hills.

Other rebels came to join him and the small group began what today is referred to as guerrilla warfare against the Syrian occupiers. A year later, in 166 BC, Mattathias died and the group chose the third of his sons, Judas Maccabeus, as his successor. The name Maccabeus is thought to derive from the Hebrew word *maqqaba*, which means hammer.

The revolt spread and the rebels increased in number to the point that they were able to challenge the Syrian troops in battle. They defeated the occupiers, first at Emmaus and then at Bethsura. Jerusalem fell to Judah and the remaining inhabitants of the city could then destroy every vestige of pagan worship. Their celebrations at this change of events are still commemorated in the annual Hanukkah festivities.

When Antiochus died, the struggle between his successors favored the Jewish rebels, who were able to exploit the international situation. The empire of the Seleucids broke up under pressure from the Egyptians and the Romans. One after another, the five sons of Mattathias led their people back to independence and, under the Maccabees, Judah was increased in size to include nearly as much land as Solomon had ruled.

201 *This illustration is taken from* Histoire de l'Ordre de la Toison d'Or *by Cardinal Guillaume Fillastre, a humanist and supporter of the anti-popes Benedict XIII and John XXIII in the late 14th and early 15th centuries. In the foreground we see the death of Mattathias; in the background, Judah Maccabee fights against Apollonius, the superintendent of the tributes sent to the land of Judah by Antiochus, then against Seron, the commander of the Syrian forces, at Beth-oron.*

THE New
TESTAMENT

HEROD THE GREAT AND THE BIRTH OF THE MESSIAH

202-203 *This is the* Madonna and Child and St. John, *a youthful work by Botticelli dated 1468 but better known as the* Madonna del Roseto. *The influence of Filippo Lippi, a Florentine master who died in 1469, is evident.*

204 *In Filippo Lippi's* Annunciation *in Palazzo Barberini, Rome, the Virgin appears composed as though she were*

already waiting to hear the first Ave Maria in the world from a sorrowful angel, almost hesitant despite his divine nature.

205 *The Magi represent the three ages of man in this symbolic and central epiphany. The illustration (circa 1440) is taken from the Book of Hours that belonged to Sir Walter Raleigh.*

The desecration of the Temple

The Roman general Pompey (Gnaeus Pompeius Magnus) was the son-in-law and rival of Julius Caesar, with whom he was associated in the First Triumvirate, together with Crassus. In 63 BC, Pompey was in Damascus with his legions after having conquered the Pontus, Armenia and Syria, and Judah was embroiled in civil war between the descendants of the Maccabees. Hyrcanus and Aristobulus, the sons of the queen, Salome Alexandra who had recently died, fought one another for the throne. Both of them turned for help to the Romans who now dominated the whole of the eastern Mediterranean. Asked to act as arbiter between the two contenders for the throne, Pompey decided in favor of Hyrcanus, but far from willing to accept this decision, Aristobulus closed himself and his army in Jerusalem. As it was Pompey's duty to impose order on the East, he was forced to lay siege to the city. It fell very quickly and Aristobulus gave himself up, but his supporters refused to surrender and hid themselves in the fort-like Temple, where they resisted for three months. To lay their war machines close to the walls of the city, the Romans had to fill in a deep ditch, and this arduous task was made all the more difficult by the defenders who attacked the soldiers at work from the top of the walls. Ironically, it was the Jewish faith that led to the Jews' downfall as Pompey realized that on the Sabbath the Jews did not fight unless they were in danger of their lives, so he had the ditch filled in only on that day. When the Romans were finally able to bring their war machines close to the walls, their soldiers could jump down and invade the Temple enclosure. Unperturbed by the advance of the Roman soldiers, the priests continued to celebrate rites and sacrifices though they were massacred as they did so. The Romans cut down anyone they came across and Hyrcanus' faction was even less tolerant. Twelve thousand people died in the episode, many of who chose to commit suicide by throwing themselves off the city walls. Pompey did not loot the Temple but dared to enter the sanctuary, which alone represented profanation. The next day he ordered the purification of the Temple and nominated Hyrcanus as the high priest and ruler of Judah. Then, after receiving payment of 10,000 talents, Pompey left Jerusalem. The Romans made Judah part of the new Roman province of Syria and used the weak-willed Hyrcanus purely as their puppet. In 60 BC Crassus joined with Julius Caesar and Pompey in forming another triumvirate, which effectively took control of the Roman Empire. He became governor of Syria, and ordered the treasure of the Temple to be looted. Later, in 53 BC, he was killed in the devastating defeat at Carrhae during a vainglorious military campaign against the Parthians. When the news of his death reached Judah, the followers of Aristobulus raised a new revolt hoping to profit from the occasion to free the country, but it went against them and 30,000 rebel Jews were sold into slavery. In 43 BC the Parthians entered Judah and placed their own candidate on the throne. This was Antigonus, the last of the Hasmonean-Maccabees. After the assassination of Caesar, in Rome in 44 BC, Mark Antony and Octavian shared power. Rome decided that the crown of Judah should be handed to Herod, the son of Antipater, who had been one of the strongest supporters of Roman power in the region.

207 In 63 BC, Pompey the Great and his soldiers desecrated Solomon's Temple in Jerusalem, massacring the priests and defenders of the holy building. The episode marked the start of the bloody period of crisis during into which, sixty years later, the Messiah was born. This image, dominated by a cruel red, was painted by the 15th century miniaturist Jean Fouquet in a French translation of Josephus' Antiquities of the Jews.

The greatness and sufferings of Herod

During his reign, Herod was like a small Jewish Augustus and is referred to as "the Great" by historians. He had taken Mariamne, the daughter of the Hasmonean queen Salome Alexandra, as his second wife, thereby relating himself to the reigning dynasty represented by Antigonus. With the help of the Romans, Herod captured Antigonus and handed him over to Mark Antony, who had him executed.

In 37 BC, one of Herod's first acts of his thirty-two year reign was to kill all the Jews who had come of age and supported his rival. Josephus describes Herod as "a warrior that no one could defeat" and a sort of Jewish Mars; he was a great horseman, hunter, archer and a spear thrower who never missed his target. And he was also a shrewd ruler; during the power struggle between Octavian on the one hand and Mark Antony and Cleopatra on the other, Herod was always on the side of the winner. He came out of every crisis with greater territory and extended powers. Augustus respected Herod's intelligence and passed him a number of Palestinian cities that had previously been wrenched from the kingdom of Judah. He also considered the idea of making Herod governor of Syria and Egypt in the name of the Roman Empire. As brave as Achilles and as cunning as Odysseus, learned and magnificent, Herod loved power as much as beauty but he had one flaw that made him vulnerable: he was pathologically suspicious. This characteristic was to a certain extent understandable in a time of continual poisonings and stabbings, and in a person who had passed his whole life surrounded by overt and masked enemies. However, it made him a victim of others' intrigues and induced him to take decisions that he would later regret bitterly.

Of his ten wives, Mariamne was "a chaste woman but rather harsh by nature" who treated her husband imperiously because she knew that he loved her to the point of thinking himself her slave. Also, proud of her Hasmonean blood, she considered Herod a low-ranking newcomer and treated both his mother and Salome, Herod's sister, with disdain. To ingratiate himself with his wife, Herod had appointed Mariamne's younger brother, the seventeen-year-old Aristobulus III, high priest. The young boy of royal descent became so popular among the Jews that the king began to fear he might rise up against him to reestablish the fallen dynasty. Consequently, Herod had the boy drowned during aquatic games held in Jericho (Hellenic ways had been introduced to all of Palestine), and the incident covered over as an accident, but neither Mariamne nor her mother was deceived and together they swore to take revenge. In the meantime, Salome's hate for the prideful queen grew. She had already tried to spite Mariamne by telling Herod that his wife was having a relationship with her own husband Joseph. Herod's reaction was to have Joseph killed, but, being infatuated with his wife, to leave her unpunished.

Some years later, Salome tried another tack. This time she corrupted the court cupbearer and convinced him to tell Herod that Mariamne had asked him to place a "love potion" (probably a poison) in the king's drink. The king ordered an investigation, which came to nothing, but by now the suspicion in his mind was too strong, and the queen was tried, condemned and put to death. However, immediately the punishment had been carried out, Herod was overwhelmed with remorse and by the doubt that he had put an innocent person to death. He began to call her name out loud and sent his servants to look for her. One day he went off into the desert in search of solitude and had to be brought back, having become feverish, by force. He was returned to his senses when he discovered the existence of other, probably true, plots, for example, the mother of Mariamne plotted to assassinate him and he reacted by having the guilty parties sentenced to death. Then Antipater, the son of his first wife, convinced him that Herod's two sons by Mariamne – Alexander and Aristobulus – intended to assassinate the king so these too were put to death after a show trial. Then came the turn of Antipater himself: the Greek advisor to the king, Nicolaus of Damascus, accused the young man of wishing to dethrone his father but this time, Herod limited himself to having his son put in prison.

Saddened, disappointed and prematurely aged by so many family tragedies, Herod fell gravely ill. He suffered from ulcers, fevers, convulsions and dropsy. Unable to withstand the physical and mental pain, he attempted to kill himself with a dagger but was prevented from doing so. This was a pity as it left him enough time for him to perpetrate another tragedy: when he learned that Antipater had attempted to escape from prison, he ordered his son to be beheaded, then, five days later, he too died. His sister Salome and her new husband, Alexas, refused to carry out Herod's last order, that of having all those young men of age around Jericho killed as soon as the king had died. His reason was that he wanted the entire country to be in mourning following his death, but that might just be a defamation put forward by his many enemies. They accused him of having stolen the throne like a fox, holding onto it like a tiger and dying like a dog, but his reign was not simply a river of blood. He had restored order to a country overwhelmed by years of confusion, he ruthlessly rid the country of the robbers that infested it, exempted the poor from paying taxes, succeeded in convincing Rome to reduce the tribute required, and increased

Temple, which had remained modest since Zerubbabel had built it five hundred years earlier. Herod had an area of 220 square yards laid down on Mount Moriah, around which a huge porticoed enclosure was built with a ceiling made of carved cedarwood. It was supported by marble Corinthian columns so large that three men could hardly encircle them with their arms. This formed the main court where money-changers had their stalls, sellers offered animals needed for sacrifices, students and teachers of Law and the Hebrew language studied, and beggars beseeched the pity of the faithful. A flight of steps led to a second level where only Jews could enter, then a ramp rose to the priests' court, where the sacrificial altar stood. The gates to these areas were lined with gold and silver, and the enormous doors of the Tem-

trade. Like his admirer and protector Mark Antony, Herod was a great builder: he founded the city of Caesarea Palaestinae and built it a port as large as that of Piraeus, which served Athens. It was the first to be built on the open sea, with two immense breakwaters that protected a large harbor, and flanked by a magnificent palace that faced out to sea.

He also built a huge palace in Jerusalem modeled on his favorite Greek and Roman architectural forms. He filled it with statues, marble, gold, mosaics and paintings, and surrounded it with gardens. To the amazement and disapproval of old Jews, he had a theater and amphitheater built in the holy city of Jerusalem for Greek-style musical and athletic competitions, and for Roman-style gladiatorial games. He lined the streets and squares of the city with statues of nudes. Finally he turned his attention to the

ple proper (70 feet high and 23 feet wide) were made of bronze. Inside the white marble walls there hung an embroidered veil of blue, purple and scarlet. In front of it stood the seven-armed candelabra, the incense altar and a table on which the priestly offering to God of unleavened bread was placed. Behind the veil lay the Holy of Holies, which in the first Temple had held the Ark of the Covenant, but which now was empty. Only the high priest was allowed to enter it, and only once a year, on the day of the Expiation.

It took eight years to build the structure, but as the people saw the marvelous construction rise, they complained that Herod must have stolen the treasure that, according to legend, had been hidden in David's tomb. A further eight years were needed to complete the decorations but, soon after it was finally ready, it was destroyed forever.

209 The smoke of sacrifices rises from King Herod's temple
in this fascinating reconstruction taken from a
monumental Life of Christ *illustrated by James Tissot*
between 1886 and 1894.

210-211 This delicately humanistic interpretation of the importance of the words of the Evangelists shows the Virgin Mary, seated in a Renaissance garden, receiving the heavenly messenger. This Annunciation *is a youthful work by Leonardo da Vinci.*

210 bottom Since the 1st century AD, the Church of the Annunciation in Nazareth, built above a group of rock-cave dwellings, has been a place of worship honoring the Virgin Mary.

212-213 Mary watches the Child; a detail from the 14th-century frescoes in the church of San Francesco in Assisi. They are partly attributed to Simone Martini.

Toward the end of his reign, in a year that experts still dispute and may have been 7 BC, a messenger from God, the archangel Gabriel, descended to the village of Nazareth in Galilee. He was looking for a young woman named Mary who had been born to parents, now elderly, named Joachim and Anne who were descended from the line of David. He found her, according to the apocryphal gospel ("Protevangelium") of St. James, as she was drawing water from the spring that can still be seen today. It lies at the extreme north of Nazareth and is named Ain sitti Myriam after her. Gabriel greeted her as being "blessed among women." The Gospel according to St. Luke places the encounter between Gabriel and Mary in the young girl's house, which was a poor, two-roomed shack that leant, as was customary, against a hill for support, and

which, at the back, had a cave in the rock. Today this is part of a church built in 1730 by the Franciscans over the remains of a Byzantine basilica that Baybars, the Sultan of Egypt, had demolished in 1263, after the Crusaders' Kingdom of Jerusalem had fallen to the Moslems. With the Moslem dominion over Jerusalem, Christians were prevented from having access to holy sites, but a host of angels supposedly lifted the birthplace of the Virgin and transported it first to Tersatto in Dalmatia, and then placed it definitively in Loreto in the Italian marches. Marches. The cave in Nazareth contains a tomb that in the Middle Ages was believed to be the burial place of St. Joseph. However, burial inside houses was completely contrary to Hebrew custom and there is no other tradition that refers to Mary's husband's resting place.

214-215 *Swarms of angels contemplate the birth of the Child in the frescoes in the lower church of St. Francis in Assisi. The naturalness of the faces is extraordinary, as is the loving Mary who watches, not a divine infant, but a crying baby, the Son of Man.*

215 *This nativity scene is taken from the* Très Belles Heures de Bruxelles *commissioned by Jean de France, duke of Berry (1340-1416). This illustrious figure was more of an art patron than a politician, and commissioned a superb collection of illuminated manuscripts of which a hundred or so have survived.*

When Joseph learned of his betrothed's pregnancy, the writers of apocryphal work claim that he "trembled all over and struck his face; he rolled on the mat and cried bitterly," and, according to an Arab legend, he wished to kill her. Reassured by another angel, he accepted the arrangements that had been made for the wedding and also the child that had been divinely conceived.

Shortly after the wedding, the couple left Nazareth for Bethlehem, which was south of Jerusalem. The Roman authorities were taking a census of the population and Joseph was obliged to register in his family's town of origin, which was also the birthplace of King David. It was a difficult trip for the young pregnant wife and, when they reached their destination, they had to be content with a stall that had been built in a cave as, owing to the census, there was no room in the inn.

That night, the sound of angels singing woke shepherds in the area and encouraged them to go to the cave where, in the light of a full moon (writes an apocryphal author) they worshipped the newborn baby that was kept warm by the breath of an ox and a donkey. It was a clear, starry, mild spring night.

Until the 4th century, Christians celebrated the birth of Jesus on 28 March, 18 April or 29 May. In the East the date was established as being 6 January (calculating thirty years from conception rather than from the birth) and called Epiphany, that is, the earthly manifestation of divinity. In the West, Jesus' birth was made coincident with a pagan festival, that of Sol Invictus (the sun god). In the 3rd AD, the cult of this god had spread throughout the Roman Empire and his annual rebirth was celebrated with the winter solstice, on 25 December.

216-217 The hand of Botticelli is recognizable in the composed devotion seen on the faces of Mary and Joseph in this detail from a Nativity *from the school of the master. Jesus' year of birth is uncertain, but most biblical scholars agree it was around 7 BC.*

218 *The adoration of the three Magi from Zoroastrian* *Persia is the subject of this illumination from* Les Petites Heures, *commissioned by Jean, duke of Berry. The tradition relating to these wise men has altered but consolidated over the centuries: for example, their number varied from two to twelve depending on the era, but fixed on three in the 6th century.*

219 *'For unto you is born this day in the city of David a Savior' (Luke 2, 11) the angels announce to the shepherds. Luke is the only one of the four gospels to relate the birth of Jesus. Note the dog barking in alarm in the bottom right corner of this vibrant illustration from the* Petites Heures.

of the Roman emperor Constantine, had a splendid basilica built there, adorned by the emperor "in truly regal fashion." Over the centuries this building has undergone many transformations and restorations until it has taken on its current appearance. An altar dedicated to the Three Kings stands in front of the stall where Mary placed her newborn son, and which is now represented by an excavation in the rock lined with white marble. The three kings were three wise men who came from faraway Persia to be present at the event that their astronomical calculations had predicted. They were guided towards Palestine by a comet and, when they arrived in Jerusalem, went to give their greetings to the infirm Herod. They told him they had made their journey to worship the "King of the Jews," who was to be born in that period.

220 Small and filled with lamps and brocade, the Crypt of the Nativity has been a place of worship since the times of St. Helena, the searcher after 'things evangelical.' On the extreme right, protected by a canopy, is the place of the crib; to the left, is the altar dedicated to the Magi.

est: this is the laconic message engraved on the silver star (a representation of the star the Magi followed) in the smallest niche in the grotto in Bethlehem.

222 *Pagan idols crumble at the passage of the Holy Family on their*
way to Egypt. This illumination is from Les Petites Heures,
commissioned by Jean, duke of Berry. Jean died in 1416; in the same
year Hermann, Jean, and Pol Limbourg, creators of many of the duke's
treasured illuminated volumes, also died, probably from the plague.

Alarmed by this strange news, which was confirmed by his priests, Herod gave the order for all children younger than two to be killed throughout the entire kingdom. Jesus evaded this massacre of the innocents because an angel appeared to Joseph in a dream telling him to flee to Egypt with his family. So Mary, Joseph and Jesus took to the road with a donkey and a small flock of goats, headed down to the sea and took the coast road to the Nile valley. According to the apocryphal narratives (more inclined to far-fetched tales than the canonical books), it was during their journey that Jesus performed his first miracles. Palm trees bowed down at his passing so that they could pick their dates without trouble, lions and leopards lay down before them, wolves walked peacefully beside the goats, and

the idols in ancient Egypt fell to pieces before them. No mention is made of where the holy family stayed, but the Coptic Christians of Egypt still worship a gigantic sycamore that stands in a garden on the edge of ancient Heliopolis, a few miles from Cairo. It is known as the Tree of the Virgin and although botanists deny it could possibly be as old as two millennia, the faithful believe that the family rested in its shade.

It seems that their stay in Egypt did not last long because when Herod died in 4 BC, the angel reappeared to Joseph to exhort him to return home, saying that the danger was over. In fact Judah was troubled by revolts under the new king, Herod's son Archelaus. He had three thousand people massacred as they protested against him in the Temple enclosure.

223 *An impassive King Herod watches over the Massacre of*
the Innocents, shown with harsh realism in a 13th-century
illumination of the French school. The episode had no
historical consequences: in Palestine at that time massacres
were frequent.

224 The Massacre of the Innocents is seen in the initial letter of this 13th-century Florentine codex of liturgical chants. Of the four evangelists, only Matthew narrates the episode, linking it to a prophecy made by Jeremiah: 'Rachel weeps for her children and refuses consolation because they are no more.'

224-225 The bodies of the 'children … of two years old and under' (Matthew 2, 16) are thrown onto a heap before the eyes of King Herod in the loggia (top left) in the frescoes of the lower church of St. Francis in Assisi.

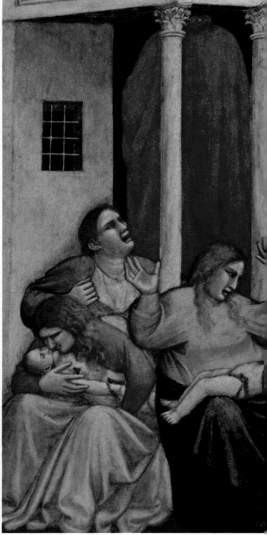

226 and 227 *Jesus' infancy was treated with*
extraordinary imagination in the Apocrypha: these two
illuminations from a late 13th-century psalter in
Cambridge, England, show the Messiah performing
bizarre miracles such as turning his playfellows into pigs
(left) and riding on a sunbeam (bottom).

Disorder and conflict persuaded Joseph to return to Nazareth rather than Bethlehem so he could return to his work as a carpenter. In the place where his workshop stood, a church was built during the Byzantine era; it is called the Church of the Nutrition and was rebuilt by the Crusaders. It was in Nazareth that Jesus "grew, and waxed strong in spirit, filled with wisdom," says St. Luke, with his brothers Jacob, Joseph, Judas, Simon, and sisters Melcha and Escha. The gospels speak of some of them and the apocrypha of others. The latter describe the infancy of the future Messiah as a series of extraordinary but not positive miracles. For example, he had children who played tricks on him put to death (but then brought them back to life); he blinded those parents who protested; and he blasted the village teacher who tried to teach him the alphabet. Finally, he treated the poor Joseph abominably, accusing him of not being his real father. Local tradition contradicts the accounts of this divine but appalling child. During the first centuries AD, they narrated that Jesus worked alongside his father; plows, supposedly made by him in Joseph's workshop, were readily displayed. This may, however, have been the invention of local relic sellers.

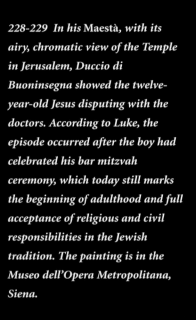

228-229 *In his* Maestà, *with its airy, chromatic view of the Temple in Jerusalem, Duccio di Buoninsegna showed the twelve-year-old Jesus disputing with the doctors. According to Luke, the episode occurred after the boy had celebrated his bar mitzvah ceremony, which today still marks the beginning of adulthood and full acceptance of religious and civil responsibilities in the Jewish tradition. The painting is in the Museo dell'Opera Metropolitana, Siena.*

At the age of twelve, Luke says, Jesus was taken to Jerusalem at the Feast of the Passover, which falls in early spring, and presented at the Temple. It was a sort of declaration of maturity as, when a Jewish male became an adult, he had to assume religious and civil duties and submit to the prescriptions of the Law. Once the rite had been performed, the family set out on the return journey to Nazareth. In the confusion of the busy roads (referring to another Passover celebration, Josephus says that three million people came to Jerusalem -- clearly an exaggeration) Joseph and Mary did not realize that Jesus

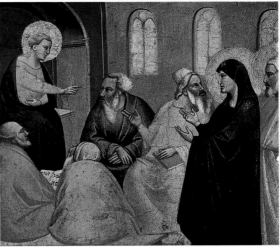

had gone missing until they arrived at the first rest stop. They thought he had remained at the back of the procession with friends and family members, but he was not to be found. Worried, they hurried back to the capital and searched for him in vain for two days and nights. Only on the third day, when they entered the Temple enclosure, did they see him seated quietly amongst the "doctors," that is, the rabbis. He was asking them questions and considering their replies, and when his mother told him off, he came back with "How is it that ye sought me? Wist ye not that I must be about my Father's business?" Joseph and Mary did not understand his reply, but this was the first manifestation of their son's vocation.

229 *In the 14th-century vision of the dispute with the doctors by Taddeo Gaddi (Giotto's 'heir'), the volumes are denser as though to contain the characters' emotionalism. The astonishment of Mary and Joseph, related by Luke, is not alluded to, as though the Messiah's superiority was already becoming apparent in the adolescent, who 'grew, and waxed strong in spirit, filled with wisdom' (Luke 2, 52).*

VT PARERET 7 PEPERIT FILIVM SVVM PRIMOGENITVM. LVCE.II. C.

IY SACTV SVV DOMINATOR DÑS 7 ANGEL ESTAMETI QVE VOS VVLTIS.MAIACHI.II.C

M INIERVSALEM VT DARENT OSTIAM PRO EO. LVCE.II. C.

ES PTERRITI 7 CAPTI SVT SAPIENTIA NVLLA EST.IN EIS.IERE.VIII.C

230-231 *One of the great works by Fra Giovanni di Fiesole (better known as Fra Angelico) was the nine main panels in the Silver Chest, originally made to hold the ex-voto offerings of the faithful in the church of the Santissima Annunziata, Florence. This is one of the master's last works, executed in 1452 just three years before his death. Painted in tempera on wood, the episodes he undoubtedly illustrated show (top) a biblical prophecy to which the evangelical occurrences (lower side) correspond. The scenes in this section range from the Mystical Wheel, with images of prophets and evangelists, to the dispute with the doctors of the law.*

THE ℙALESTINE OF JESUS

232 *Christ's earthly life has almost ended but the* Eucharist *in the Silver Chest, by Fra Angelico (1452), philologically follows the dignified emotionalism of the version by St. John. The biblical reference in this panel is the prophecy made in Ezekiel 39, 17: '… I do sacrifice for you, even a great sacrifice upon the mountains of Israel, that ye may eat flesh, and drink blood.'*

233 *In an outburst of pain, the will of God the Eternal has been fulfilled. No more than seventy years separate the late work by Fra Angelico from this disturbing* Deposition *by Rosso Fiorentino (1521). It is one of the most pitiless representations of human anguish and desperation, and revolves around the striking grimace of Christ's lips, pulled into an almost ironical smile.*

234 This aerial view shows the bends of the River Jordan in the fertile plain that stretches from the southern shore of the Sea of Galilee (today Lake Tiberias) seen in the top left corner. This region was the setting for one of Jesus' first sermons and where he selected the first apostles.

234-235 Painted between 1469 and 1480, this delicate, almost ethereal Baptism of Christ *is part of the rather limited pictorial output of Andrea del Verrocchio, in collaboration with his pupil Leonardo di Credi. Verrocchio preferred to dedicate himself to sculpture.*

The Bible tells us nothing of the youth of Jesus, and the story of his life continues with the meeting between him and John the Baptist that occurred, according to St. Luke, in the fifteenth year of the reign of Emperor Tiberius, therefore in AD 28 or 29.

Like the prophets that had gone before him, John wore a camel skin tied around his waist and fed on wild honey and locusts. He lived in the desert and preached on the banks of the Jordan where he celebrated a peculiar sort of purification ceremony: he made those who came to him confess their sins, then he made them enter the river in a symbolic gesture of washing away their sins. He censured the corruption and wickedness of the times, and warned that the day of judgment and the coming of the Kingdom of God was near. Jesus came to John and was baptized – that is to say, purified – together with others but, as the ceremony occurred, "heaven opened" and a voice was heard saying "Thou art my beloved son in whom I am well pleased." According to tradition, the baptism of Jesus took place at Beth-Hogla on the left bank of the Jordan. Since the first centuries AD, pilgrims have come here to bathe on the evening before Epiphany. In 1172 a traveler named Theodoric saw a crowd of 60,000 people all holding flaming torches as they waited on the bank for the sun to rise before they entered the water. This same ceremony was still practiced by Russians and Greeks Orthodox Christians during the 20th century.

236-237 In the first half of the 17th century, Guercino
painted Salomé reluctant to receive Herod's macabre
reward, whereas her mother can be seen satisfied,
emerging from the darkness. Although he feared the
increasing influence of the Baptist over the people,
Herod is saddened by the event but was unable to draw
back, having sworn in public to satisfy any wish of the
girl for having danced so well.

At this time Galilee was governed by the tetrarch Herod Antipas, the son of Herod the Great. On the shore of the Sea of Galilee, he had founded the city of Tiberias in honor of the Roman emperor, his protector. He had made the city his capital and filled it with foreigners, beggars and opportunists of all kinds. When the foundations of the first buildings were being dug, an ancient cemetery had been discovered with the result that practicing Jews refused to settle in there as they considered it to be an impure place. The tetrarch had married Herodias, his niece, with whom he had fallen passionately in love. This arrangement was viewed by Jews as incest and scandalized the orthodox, and John the Baptist in particular criticized Herod and Herodias heavily. Herod therefore had John arrested and shut up in the fort of Machaerus that had been built by his father in one of the wildest areas in Perea to the east of the Dead Sea. Today the ruins can still be seen. However, to Herodias John's imprisonment was not enough: she wanted the man who had called her a prostitute to die. She succeeded in this through the beauty and grace of Salome, her daughter by her first marriage. The enchanting girl danced for Herod and so pleased the tetrarch that he promised to grant her any wish she made. Persuaded by her mother, Salome asked for the head of John the Baptist and, to hold good to his promise, Herod reluctantly felt bound to oblige. John was beheaded in Machaerus and his head was brought to Tiberias and presented to the triumphant Herodias on a silver plate.

238-239 *The Mount of Temptation stands in the Judean desert north of the Dead Sea. It was on this 'very high' peak that the Tempter promised Jesus the kingdoms of the world. It was not the first temptation, but, Matthew writes, it was only after this final refusal that Satan left Christ.*

239 top *This illustration in the Breviary of Isabella the Catholic (Flemish, late 15th century) epitomizes the temptations of Christ: foreground, Satan asks Jesus to change the rock into bread; top right, he offers Him the kingdoms of the world; left, he urges Jesus to throw himself from the top of the Temple.*

239 bottom *Satan is shown as a grotesque, deformed demon in this miniature taken from a 15th-century German* Life of Christ. *In Matthew 4, 2-3 the artful Tempter approached Christ after He had fasted for forty days and was suffering from hunger.*

Meanwhile Jesus had gone into the arid, mountainous region that lies between Jerusalem and the Dead Sea to fast and meditate for forty days. Here Satan tempted Jesus by taking him to the top of a mountain from where he showed him "all the kingdoms of the world," promising them to Jesus if he would only worship Satan. This place is now identified as a peak that overlooks Jericho, which is now called Gebel Qaruntul (Mount of the Forty Days). One of the many caves on the mountains is believed to have been the one where Jesus lived during this period and has been transformed into a chapel. In the 12th century, when the Crusaders had conquered Palestine, a religious order called the Brothers of the Quarantine established itself there and the cave was frescoed with the scene of the Temptation. Today the vestiges of this fresco can still just be seen.

"Being full of the Holy Ghost," as St. Luke says, after his stint in the desert, Jesus returned to Galilee and began his preaching, but although he was respected elsewhere, in his own town of Nazareth he aroused only ill-feeling. As everyone knew him, they could not believe that the son of a carpenter could be the messenger of God, as he proclaimed himself to be. The indignation of his fellow-countrymen was so great that they "led him unto the brow of the hill whereon their city was built that they might cast him down headlong. But passing through the midst of them, he went his way," almost as though he were invisible.

Gebel el Qafseh (the Mount of the Precipice) is one of the two summits that lie to the south of Nazareth, separated by a deep and narrow gorge. Two enormous blocks of rock form a parapet that drops away into the gorge where stand the remains of a monastery built in the 11th century and abandoned after the Moslem conquest of Palestine in 1187.

Leaving hostile Nazareth, Jesus headed toward the Sea of Galilee, today called Lake Tiberias. Here, he made a miraculous catch appear to the fishermen of Capernaum after they had spent an entire day fishing in vain, and found in them his first disciples: Simon, who was called Peter, Andrew, James and John. Jesus stayed in Peter's house where he healed the sick and possessed. "Crowds gathered to see him" from the surrounding villages, and Jesus preached and performed miracles. One day, as he was crossing the lake by boat, he calmed a rising storm; on another occasion in Canaan, he healed the son of a Roman centurion though the sick boy was lying in Capernaum.

240 The pale buildings of Tiberias on the eastern shore of the Sea of Galilee where the city was built in AD 20 by Herod Antipas, the son of Herod the Great. In ancient Capernaum, a few miles to the north, Jesus performed several miracles at the start of his preaching.

240-241 *In 1481-82 Domenico Ghirlandaio painted this* superb Vocation of Peter and Andrew *in the Sistine Chapel in 'modern' style but with references to Flemish painting.*

242-243 *Jesus calls Peter and Andrew, his first two apostles, to him in this dignified 17th-century interpretation by Bernardo Strozzi.*

Invited to a wedding feast in Capernaum, he was asked by his mother Mary to perform the most profane, but the kindest, of his miracles: he turned water into wine so that the guests could continue to celebrate the marriage. Antonino of Piacenza, an Italian pilgrim who passed through Canaan in 570, recounted that he had sat at the same table as Jesus had during the wedding party, and, like a good tourist, he carved names on the stone table, inexplicably, not his own but those of his parents. He was also shown two of the six amphoras that had held the water that had been turned into wine. It is surprising, and also illustrative of the huge trade in relics that began during the Byzantine era, that the table that Antonino referred to was found in Greece in 1885 among the ruins of a church in Elatea. Carved in Greek letters of the 6th or 7th century could be read "This stone comes from Canaan in Galilee where Our Lord changed the water into wine."

Jesus made several journeys from Capernaum. He spent Passover in the year 27 in Jerusalem where he healed a lame man near the Pool of Bethesda, which can be seen beneath the crypt of the Church of St. Anne.

244-245 and 245 The turning of water into wine at the wedding in Cana is illustrated here by Duccio di Buoninsegna in his Maestà *(1308-11) in the Duomo, Siena, and in a mosaic in the church of Sant'Apollinare Nuovo, Ravenna. Biblical scholars have long debated the episode. It was a 'temporal' miracle, i.e., it had no spiritual or divine aims; the most plausible explanations are that it was a benevolent gesture to satisfy human weakness or an act of kindness to his mother, who had asked for his help.*

246 *Jesus restores sight to the blind man in a classically inspired interpretation by Eustache le Sueur (1616-55). One Jesus' first miracles, it scandalized the Pharisees because Jesus performed it on the Sabbath, thereby breaking one of the most important precepts in the Jewish tradition.*

247 *This spirited representation of Christ resuscitating the son of the widow of Nain is also by Eustache le Sueur. It was during this period that the 'great multitude' of Jesus' followers began to form as a result of his spontaneous and anti-traditionalist miracles.*

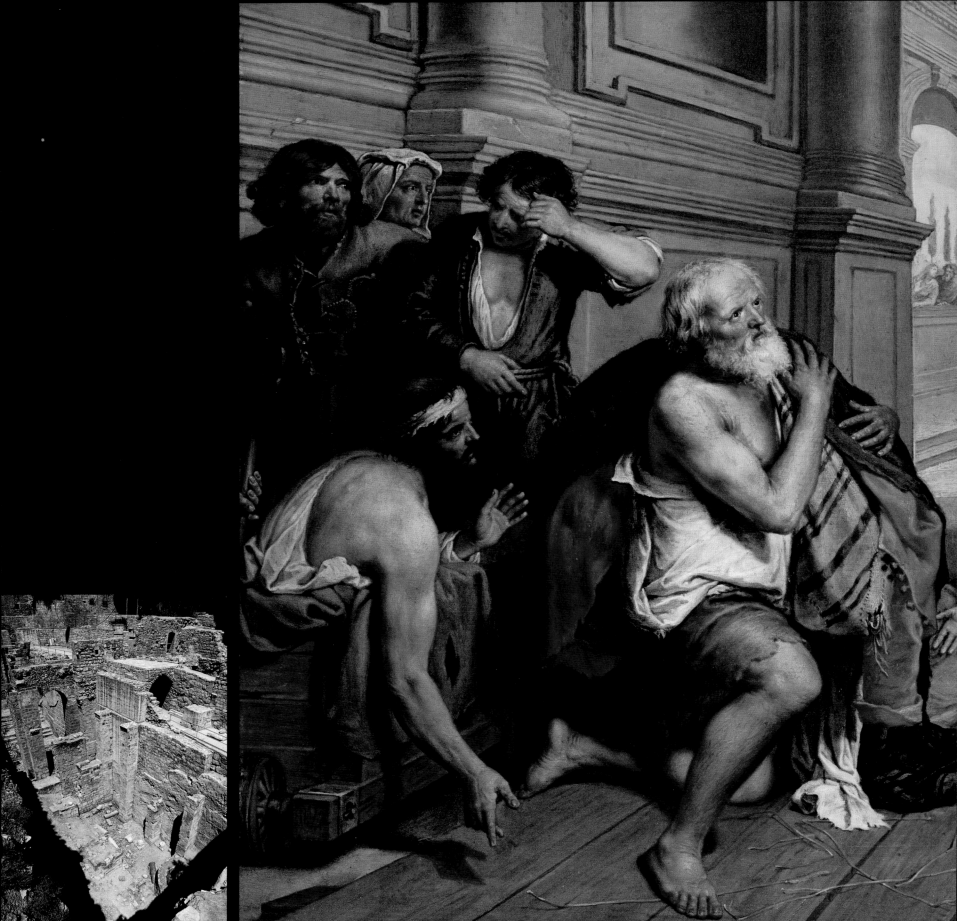

P. VLLINT. f.

'Blessed are the poor in spirit'

When he returned to Galilee, his followers had turned into a multitude and he, to have a few days of peace, withdrew to the hills with a small group of companions, who were later to be known as the Twelve Apostles. But the crowds began to search Jesus out and, when they found him on the slopes of a hill that may have been Kurn Hattin (where in 1187 Saladin inflicted a dreadful defeat on the Crusaders), he preached to them the Beatitudes or the Sermon on the Mount. On a second occasion Jesus went in search of peace in a desert area near Bethsaida, but also there the crowds would not leave him alone. The crowds were so large that he was obliged to feed them by turning five loaves and five fishes into enough food to feed five thousand people. In that place, over the rock on which he placed the modest refreshments, a church was built from which pilgrims used to remove bits of stone from the walls as talismans against sickness. Elated by the miracle, the crowd wanted to proclaim Jesus king, but he refused. Jesus' next miracle was when he walked on the water, and Peter, wishing to emulate him, began to sink as he did not have the necessary faith.

250 *Surrounded by disciples, Jesus lists the Beatitudes:
'Blessed are the poor in spirit…' in the* Sermon on the
Mount *by Fra Angelico. The group of disciples closest to
Christ – the twelve apostles – stands out against Christ's
ever growing number of devotees who followed him
wherever he went in Galilee.*

250-251 *The octagonal drum of the Church of the Sermon
(in Tabgha, just south of Capernaum) alludes to the eight
Beatitudes. The hill where the church is built is
traditionally thought to be the site of Jesus' sermon and of
one of his most sensational miracles: the feeding of the five
thousand.*

…ANIB VTQVINISDVHPISCIBVSVOSVP EO BIN…

IC XC

252-253 *The mosaics in St. Mark's Basilica, Venice, show Jesus multiplying the fish and bread to feed the crowd. Mark's reckoning was that there were 5,000 people along the shore of the Sea of Galilee.*

252 bottom *Mosaics with naturalistic and cultural themes were discovered in Tabgha in 1932 on the site of a 4th-century Byzantine basilica. One of them was this extraordinary and touching allusion to Christ's miracles.*

SIC͞I͞BO DE T ECTI VŌ PSALMI·LEGE
P PͪETIS.

At this time Jesus heard the disturbing news of the death of John the Baptist, and also that Herod Antipas intended to come down hard on Jesus himself. So he decided to go away for a while and traveled to Tyre in Phoenicia. He wished to remain anonymous, but he was recognized there by a woman who convinced him to heal her sick daughter. A few months later he returned to Galilee, where he met up with the apostles near Gaulanitide (the Golan Heghts region) at Cae-

sarea Philippi, which lies below Mount Hermon, on the banks of the river Jordan. Here he climbed a "high mountain" taking with him just Peter, James and John; they saw Jesus turn almost evanescent, and his clothes become as shining and white as snow. Then two figures appeared next to Jesus, those of Moses and Elijah, and the three disciples prostrated themselves astounded and terrified. This event is known as the Transfig-uration in which Jesus' divinity was revealed

*254 A 9th-century church was built over the ruins of a
Byzantine basilica that stood on the top of Mount Tabor in
the Yzreel valley close to Nazareth. This small rise has
traditionally been identified as the site of the
Transfiguration of Christ though the Gospels suggest a
somewhat higher peak.*

*255 Between 1438 and 1447 Fra Angelico painted a great
number of frescoes in the new monastery of San Marco,
Florence, in particular over the entrances to the monks'
cells. One of his later ones was this austere and simple*
Transfiguration, *in which Christ's expression makes him
seem strikingly detached.*

Commentators believe that the "high mountain" could only be a crag on Mount Hermon. The mountain itself is 9186 feet high and can be reached in just a few hours walk from Caesarea Philippi. But tradition since the early Christian centuries has it that the episode took place on another mountain, less high (only 1970 feet) and much more distant. This was Mount Tabor, which lies between Nazareth and the Jordan in Galilee. Here, on the fortified peak that offered last resistance against the Romans of the Jews' under Josephus (who was then obliged to enter the service of the winners), the Basilica of the Transfiguration was built in the 4th century. It had a flight of 4,340 steps built at the instigation of St. Helena, but all trace of this now has gone. After the First Crusade, a Benedictine monastery was established so that the basilica could be rebuilt but this is now in ruins. Between 1210 and 1212, when the mountain was once more under Islamic control, the Moslems filled the nave with rubble and then built a large tower over the top of it and walls around it. In 1228, when Emperor Frederick II (the Holy Roman Emperor) purchased Nazareth and Mount Tabor from the ruler of Egypt, Malek el Kamel (often referred to as Al-Kamil Muhammud), another order of monks arrived – the Hungarian Brothers – who found only the crypt intact. They built a smaller church in front of the crypt, using the stone of the previous construction. In 1254, St. Louis, the king of France, prayed here, but nine years later Sultan Baybars destroyed the church definitively. Today a 19th-century basilica can be seen there.

256-257 *In Titian's version of the Transfiguration (1560) in the church of San Salvatore, Venice, dazzling light dissolves the proportions and shapes of the bodies. The faces of Christ and the prophets in this highly charged and intellectual interpretation are almost dissolved, removing attention almost completely from the observers.*

257 *Enclosed between two massive bell-towers and behind the elegant Neo-Romanesque arch, the façade of the Church of the Transfiguration is a superb 19th-century construction. The building stands on the site of a 4th-century Byzantine basilica and is reached by a flight of 4,340 steps built on the wishes of St. Helena, mother of Emperor Constantine.*

The Messiah in Jerusalem

Having returned once more to Capernaum, Jesus left in autumn, never to return. He went south to Jerusalem to celebrate the Festival of the Tabernacles, which fell at the end of October. He then passed to Samaria, where he was poorly welcomed, and settled for a while in Bethany just outside the capital in the house of three siblings: Lazarus, Martha and Mary. From here he rode a young donkey that had never been mounted before into Jerusalem, followed by the Twelve Apostles. For some time he continued to stay in Bethany, going into the Holy City to preach. On one of these visits, using a hemp whip, he chased out of the Temple enclosure the traders who sold animals for the sacrifices, and overturned the tables of the moneychangers, censuring them for having turned "the house of my Father" into an impure place. These gestures and Jesus' preaching provoked the anger and worry of the priests, who threatened to have him stoned.

For a while Jesus left Jerusalem to take the Word of God to the region of Perea that lay on the other side of the Jordan where John the Baptist had preached. But only a few days had passed when he received a message from Martha and Mary that their brother Lazarus was seriously ill, and the request for Jesus to return and heal him.

258 *'Behold, thy king cometh unto thee ... and riding upon an ass.' This was the prophecy in Zechariah 9, 9 regarding Jesus' entry into Jerusalem. Fra Angelico faithfully follows Matthew's narration of the scene, showing the olive branches and cloaks the crowd placed on the ground.*

258-259 *An orderly Renaissance-style Jerusalem awaits Christ in this clear-cut representation by Fra Angelico. It is calculated that the city, partially rebuilt by Herod in about 37 BC, had 40,000 inhabitants in Jesus' lifetime.*

*260-261 Seen from the southeast, the Temple court bounds
the east side of the old city of Jerusalem. Solomon's Temple
and, later, Herod's Temple were built on the site where the
marvelous Dome of the Rock (Omar's Mosque), seen on the
right, now stands. To the left of the vast platform stood the
original city, known as the City of David.*

262-263 Christ chases the dealers
out of the temple in Giotto's version
of the event. In this fresco in the
Scrovegni Chapel the balance of the
composition and the attention of
the observer - like that of the figures
portrayed - hinges around Jesus'
action. Christ is on the point of
striking a money-changer with
a brawling punch, as has often
been noted.

264-265 A birds-eye view shows the
full size of the Temple court.
Restored around 20 BC by Herod the
Great, the Temple was a larger
reconstruction of the earlier Temple
built by Solomon in the 10th century
BC. All that remains of Herod's
version is the massive walls that
enclose the area. Left, we see the
Western Wall, more commonly but
less appropriately known as the
Wailing Wall, where the Jews
commemorate the final destruction
of the Holy of Holies by Emperor
Titus in 70 AD.

Jesus stayed some days more in Perea before returning to Judea, telling his apostles that Lazarus was already dead. And, in fact, when the party reached Bethany, Lazarus had already been buried for four days. But Jesus had the rock in front of the tomb rolled away and called to Lazarus. At Jesus' voice, Lazarus got to his feet, wrapped in funerary bandages, and walked out of the tomb.

The tomb was located just outside of Bethany in a place called Lazarim, which, in Arabic, became El Azarieh. It is formed by a vestibule with a long flight of steps, then a second, narrower flight of just three steps that lead into a second small square room mea-suring about 6 feet on each side. This was where Lazarus was buried. It was transformed into a chapel, with an altar and marble lining (since disappeared); in the 12th century, during the Crusader Kingdom of Jeruslaem, a church was built above it, in which the Latin patriarchs of Palestine liked to be buried. In the 16th century, after the church had been destroyed, the Moslems replaced it with a mosque and the entrance to the tomb was walled up. The story ends with the fact that at the start of the 17th century, an Italian Franciscan, Angelo of Messina, paid a large sum of money to get permission for the current entrance to be opened.

266-267 In the Resurrection of Lazarus *(1303-05) painted by Giotto in the Scrovegni Chapel in Padua, the master suffuses the scene with an emotional intensity that only the hieratic, almost imperious, Christ seems untouched by.*

267 Bethany is believed to have been the site of Lazarus' tomb. In the 4th century a Byzantine basilica, later destroyed by an earthquake, stood here but was rebuilt several times up till the Crusader era.

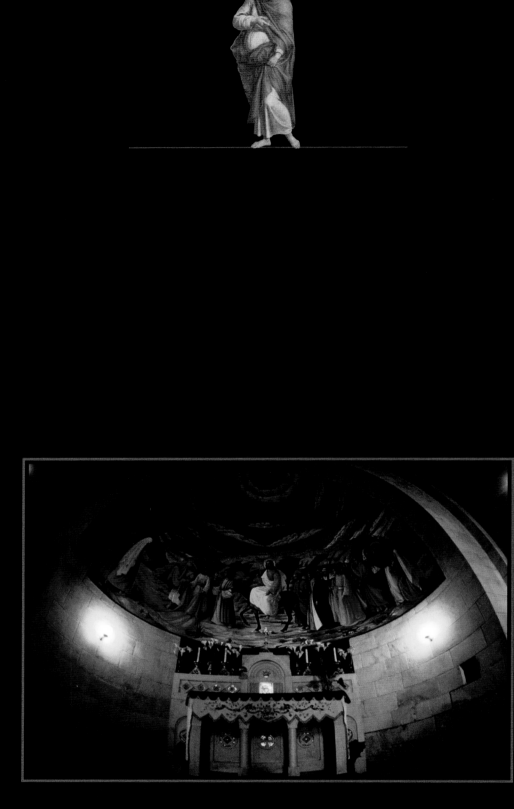

268 *Inside the church of Lazarus, a dome with a fresco showing the entry of Jesus into Jerusalem looks down on a 9th-century altar. The Arab name of the town – el-Azarya – creates a direct connection with the name Lazarus and the connection is supported by the name Lazarium mentioned by medieval pilgrims.*

268-269 *Clearly reflecting the styles of 17th-century Spanish painting, this* Resurrection of Lazarus *by Léon Bonnat, a Frenchman (1833-1922), contrasts the world of man with the world of light incarnated by Christ.*

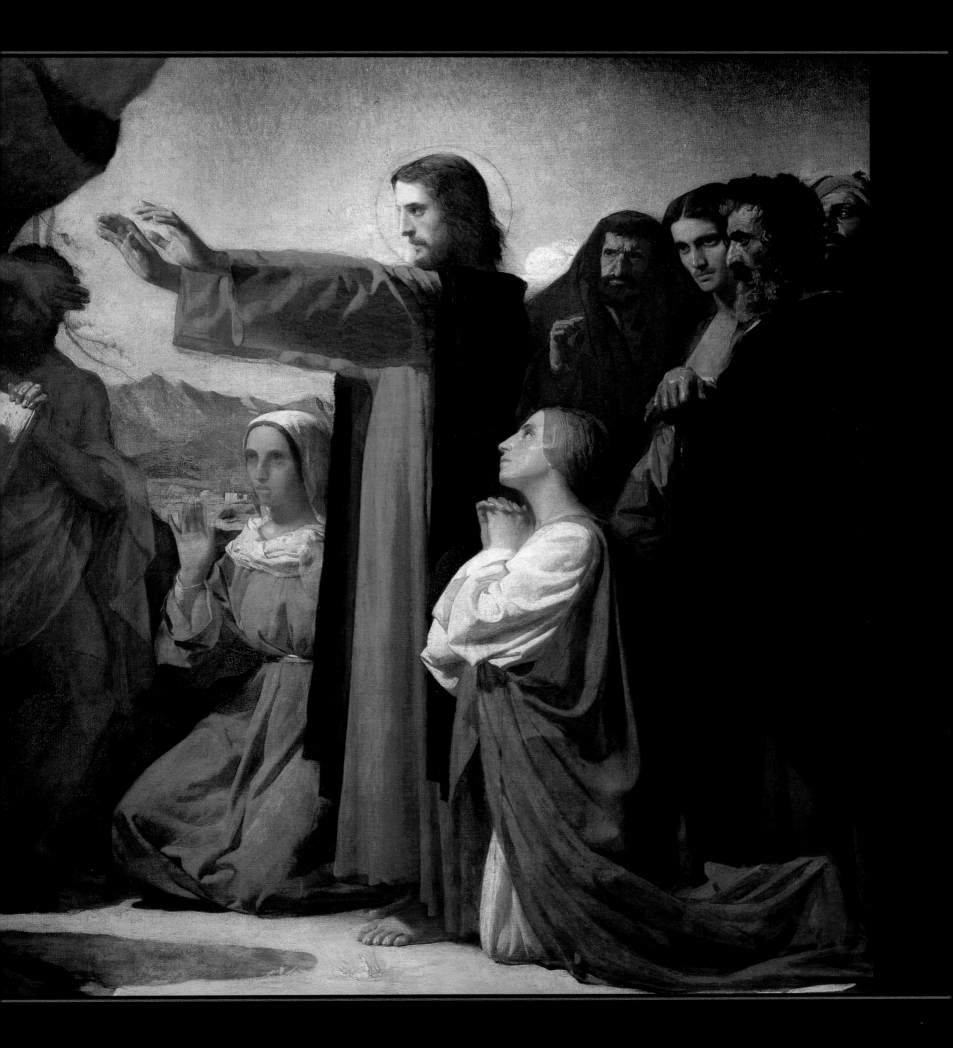

The Last Supper

Jesus returned to Perea for a last journey of preaching, passing through the village of Ephraim in the north. The story of the miraculous resurrection of Lazarus spread, but put fear into the hearts of the priests and doctors of the Law, who considered Jesus a dangerous subversive and were in favor of having him arrested. Jesus stayed away for some months but returned to Bethany a few days before Passover. His return was celebrated with a banquet in the house of a man named Simon at which Lazarus, Martha and Mary were present. To show her devotion to Jesus, Mary took a pound of essence of nard – a very strong and costly perfume – with which she washed his feet, then wiped them with her hair. The gesture aroused the indignation of the apostles, who believed it to be a waste of money, but Jesus appreciated it as a sign of love for him.

Another meal was prepared in Jerusalem for the day before Passover in the house of another Mary, the sister of Peter, and the mother of the future evangelist Mark (at least, according to tradition, but the gospels do not mention the name of the owner of the house). This was to be the Last Supper that Jesus shared with the Twelve Apostles, one of whom was to betray him. At the extreme south of Mount Zion, just outside Zion Gate in the walls of Jerusalem, a small church was built around the Cenacolo and, in the 4th century, a large basilica that has several times been destroyed and rebuilt. From the 11th century, it was said that beneath the lower room in the Cenacolo, where Jesus washed the feet of the Apostles, the tomb of King David was discovered. The place remained entrusted to the Franciscans until 1551, when the Ottoman sultan Suleiman the Magnificent ordered their expulsion and the church was turned into a mosque.

270 His time has arrived: in this fresco by Pietro Lorenzetti (first half of the 14th century) in the lower church of St. Francis in Assisi, Jesus gathers the apostles around him for the Last Supper. *This is one of the episodes in the Gospels to have most profoundly influenced Western culture, to the point of having become a symbol of betrayal, pardon and detachment from the world.*

271 top In his representation of the Washing of the Feet (first half of the 15th century), Fra Angelico emphasizes the natural behavior of the onlookers. Right, Simon Peter tries to stop Jesus but receives the reproach, 'If I wash thee not, thou hast no part with me' (John 13, 8).

271 bottom On the back of the Maestà (1308-11) by Duccio di Buoninsegna in the Duomo of Siena, 26 panels are dedicated to the Passion. In this section Jesus takes his leave of his apostles in a composition finally free from Byzantine precision and invested with the innovative Gothic style, of which Duccio was one of the first masters.

The Eucharist

272 The Cenacolo's subdued architecture was the work of 12th-century Crusaders who sought to enclose Mount Zion in Jerusalem, which a later tradition identifies as the site of the Last Supper.

272-273 The Last Supper was one of the most important works of art in the Italian Renaissance. It was painted using a combination of techniques (not fresco) by Leonardo between 1495-98. Recently restored and stabilized, this masterpiece originally began to deteriorate in the 16th century.

The Garden of Gethsemane

274 The place where Jesus was arrested – the Garden of Gethsemane – is today occupied by the 20th-century church of All Nations, consecrated to the supranational values of religious faith. Standing at the foot of the Mount of Olives, this area was already venerated in the 1st century.

275 In this touching panel in the Silver Chest (1452), partly attributed to Fra Angelico, Jesus is shown at the supreme moment of doubt, when he asks the Father to 'Take away this cup from me' (Mark 14, 36). Bottom, the disciples 'sleeping for sorrow' (Luke 22, 45).

After the Last Supper, Jesus left Jerusalem with his eleven faithful disciples (Judas had left the meal to betray Jesus) and took the road towards Bethany. The party stopped at the Mount of Olives in a place called Gethsemane ('the olive mill') where it was Jesus' custom to stop to pray. It was night and cold, but Jesus walked through the trees followed only by Peter, James and John. The others lay down to sleep in the mill. This was the night of Jesus' agony: "Father, if it be thy will, take this cup away from me. Yet not my will but thine be done" said Jesus sweating blood. An angel came down from Heaven to give him comfort but shortly after a crowd of soldiers arrived led by Judas. Judas kissed Jesus on the cheek to indicate to the soldiers that he was the one to be arrested.

Some of the disciples tried to resist and Peter cut off the ear of one of the soldiers, but Jesus intervened, ordered them to lay down their arms and allowed himself to be taken away. In this place too a church was built in the 4th century. It was called the Church of the Agony, but it too was destroyed before being rebuilt and enlarged during the Crusades. In an enclosed garden nearby there are two enormous olive trees, whose trunks measure 26 feet and 36 feet in circumference; their age means they seem to be made more of rock than wood. "These are the most revered trees in the world," says a Palestinian guide piously, "as, even if they do not date from the time of Christ, they are certainly the descendants of those trees that were present at his prayer and agony."

The arrest of Jesus marked the start of the Passion, the traditional path of which has been followed for centuries by millions of pilgrims. The prisoner was led first to the house of the former high priest Annas, then to that of Caiaphas, the high priest at that time, where Jesus was interrogated and flogged. In the 4th century the column to which Jesus was bound used to be shown but this was destroyed when Jerusalem was taken and devastated by the Persians in 614.

The place where Pontius Pilate's praetorium (official residence) stood -- where Jesus was taken after being sentenced to death by the Sanhedrin, the supreme Jewish legislative and judicial assembly, which probably met in the house of Caiaphas -- is found in the oldest section of Antony's Fort, next to the Temple. Herod had built it using "all the resources of his genius," according to Josephus. The monumental three-span gateway opened onto what was both a fort and a palace.

276 bottom In the scene of the arrest of Jesus by Duccio, the tension reaches its culmination with Judas' kiss, the moment that marks the beginning of the Passion. This work earned the master a great sum of money and was enthusiastically received by the inhabitants of Siena.

277 Three years before Duccio painted the Maestà, Giotto had frescoed the scene of Judas' kiss in a pathos-filled scene in the Scrovegni Chapel, Padua. The composition of the later work was almost a mirror image of Giotto's interpretation.

The trial and sentence

278 *Making skilful and exuberant use of color,
as in the* Maestà, *Duccio di Buoninsegna illustrated
the* Passion of Christ *from a 'historicizing' standpoint,
paying careful attention to shading and clothing details.
Here Jesus is taken to the house of Caiaphas (discovered
in a series of buildings partially carved out of the rock
of Mount Zion), suffers the insults of the Pharisees,
is taken to Herod, and, finally, is whipped on Pontius
Pilate's orders.*

279 top *Under the eyes of Pontius Pilate, Jesus is crowned with
thorns, being punished, according to the Gospels, with what the
Roman prefect of Judea considered the maximum penalty for a
man not found guilty of any crime.*

279 bottom *Pilate gives in to the demands of the crowd and
'washes his hands' in a gesture of almost universal symbolism.
Nothing is known of the Roman's later life, but certain apocrypha
claim he converted to Christianity and suffered martyrdom.*

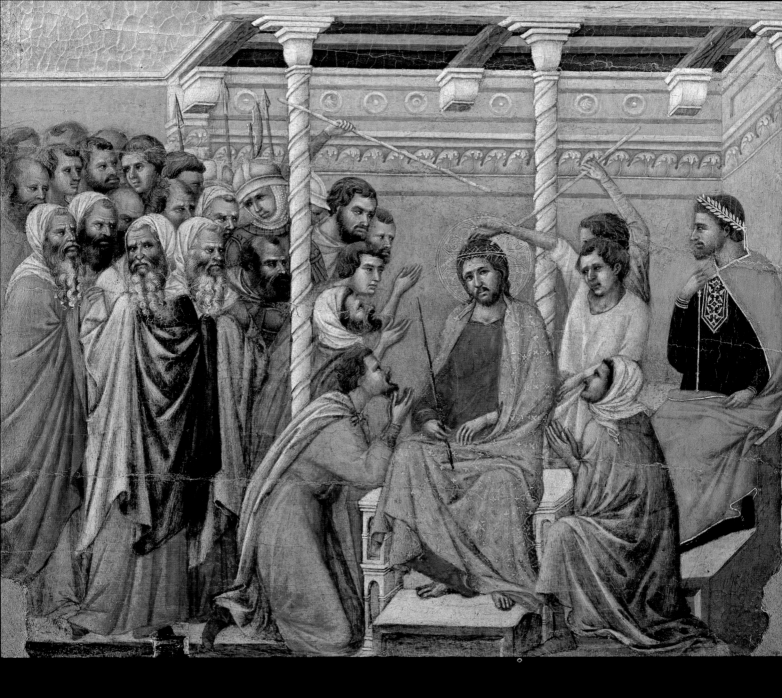

280 and 281 *The disconcerting art of Caravaggio – who portrayed the human and even brutal dimension of the divine – produced these two interpretations of the* Flagellation of Christ *in 1607. The relationship between the work and the life of the artist is still discussed: tormented and ill-fated, the previous year the painter had fled Rome after killing a man for a senseless reason.*

From the Praetorian to Calvary

The central span of the gateway still stands and is called the Ecce Homo (Behold the Man!) Arch; it is the starting point for the Via Dolorosa (Way of Sorrow) or Via Crucis (Way of the Cross). When administrative needs required the presence of the Roman Prosecutor for Judea in Jerusalem, who at that time was Pontius Pilate, he resided in the palace. Otherwise his habitual residence was in Caesarea Maritima.

Fourteen stations mark the journey Jesus made to Calvary. Strangely, it was not local tradition in the early Christian centuries that established the route but devotional custom during the Crusader period. The first to reconstruct the path that Jesus followed

was John of Wurzburg in 1165, but he went the wrong way as he started out from Mount Zion.

In the following century, a text written between 1228 and 1231 – l'*Estat de la Citez de Ihérusalem* – indicated a route that is very similar to the current one, and around 1280 first mention was made of "a caravan of western pilgrims" on the Way of the Cross. The number of stations varied: in the 16th century there were twelve, in the 17th century the number dropped to ten and then to eight, and it was only in the 18th century that it rose definitively to fourteen, each one commemorated with a chapel and inscriptions.

282 and 283 The result of the collaboration between miniaturists Jean le Noir and Jacquemart de Hesdin, the Petites Heures belonging to the art patron Jean, duke of Berry, dates from the last years of the 15th century. The elegance of the work is seen in the final moments of the Passion, particularly in the characters' faces and body language. The site of the Crucifixion – the bare hill called

Golgotha (from the Hebrew gulgoleth, 'skull') – lay outside Jerusalem's walls at the time of Christ but was enclosed within the defenses twenty years after the Resurrection. In the 2nd century, Emperor Hadrian tried to erase the memory of the site by building the forum of Aelia Capitolina over it but only succeeded in marking the location of the events for posterity.

284 On Good Friday the narrow Via Dolorosa in the Old City of Jerusalem is filled by the procession that follows the 14 Stations of the Cross to the Holy Sepulcher. The number of stations has varied over the centuries and only settled on 14 during the 18th century.

284-285 Devotion and emotion are written on the face of this worshiper during the Easter celebrations in Jerusalem. The first six stations on the Via Crucis lie within the Muslim quarter of the Old City; the next three are outside the Church of the Holy Sepulcher, and the remaining five inside. The final one is of course the site of the tomb.

Jesus' earthly existence ended in the place called Golgotha in Hebrew and Calvary in Latin. It is a bare, rounded rocky outcrop that lies just outside the walls of Jerusalem built by Herod the Great. It was not particularly assigned for use as a place of execution as the Jews had no special place for this function. In a small valley Joseph of Arimathea had excavated a family tomb, and it was here that Jesus's body was buried as soon as it was taken down from the Cross.

When Christianity began to spread throughout the Roman Empire and Calvary became a place of worship, Emperor Hadrian decided to turn Jerusalem into a pagan city and to erase every trace of Jewishness and every sanctuary of Christianity. He had rubble from an enclosure wall spread over Cal-

vary and then planted a wood consecrated to Jupiter and Venus over the top. This profanation, considered by exegetes as a sign of the authenticity of the place in which the Crucifixion took place, in fact only served to protect it from abuse. With the triumph of Christianity in the 4th century, St. Helena (the mother of Emperor Constantine) put the entire garrison of Roman soldiers in Jerusalem, helped by local volunteers, to work to remove Hadrian's wood and rubble. Her son, the emperor, then ordered the construction of the grandest basilica "worthy of the most venerated place in the world" as he wrote in a letter to St. Macarius, the

bishop of Jerusalem. The rock that contained the tomb of Christ was removed from the side of the hill and rounded, then a majestic monument was erected around it crowned by a dome; Calvary was enclosed but also left uncovered and cut into the form of a cube. The magnificent church was lined with mosaics and ornaments but was destroyed by the Persian army under King Chosroes when it took the city in 614. It was rebuilt, but its former splendor could not be restored. The Moslems respected the new building until in 1009 Caliph Hakem ordered the demolition of the Holy Sepulcher and all Christian temples and shrines in Palestine. The rock containing the tomb of Christ was partially demolished and what was left of the crumbling walls. However, in 1020 the same Hakem allowed Christians to celebrate Mass there and, eleven years later, his successor Daher el-Aziz permitted the church to be reconstructed.

When this news reached Europe, thousands of pilgrims hurried to Jerusalem taking large sums of money to pay for the construction work that began in 1042.

A century later the Crusader kings of Jerusalem wanted to make the buildings as magnificent as Constantine's basilica had been. Between 1140 and 1149 they constructed another church, but over the centuries this has undergone restoration, renovation and transformation so that it is now almost unrecognizable from its original appearance.

286 The faithful kneel to touch the stone of Golgotha in Calvary Chapel, the eleventh station on the Via Crucis, which was built over the place the Cross was raised.

286-287 In the Crucifixion scene on the Silver Chest, Fra Angelico placed the emphasis on Christ's tormentors, illustrating in detail the pain of the centurion kneeling on the right, who, frightened by the event, 'glorified God' (Luke 23, 47).

288-289 Employing a less intellectual and more pathos-
filled tone than in the subjects on which he had worked
for the Medici court, and which had made him famous,
in 1490-92 Sandro Botticelli painted the Agony of
Christ. His clearly outlined figures, rather like sculptures,
of the pious women, Mary and the Magdalene, are
gathered round the lifeless body of Jesus with saints
Peter, John, Jerome, and Paul.

290 Just inside the church of the Holy Sepulcher, the faithful
and pilgrims worship the Unction Stone on which Jesus' body
was prepared for burial with perfumed oils and ointments.

290-291 At the end of the fifteenth century, Andrea Mantegna
painted this striking perspective view of Christ which is made
more sorrowful by the depiction of His bleeding stigmata.

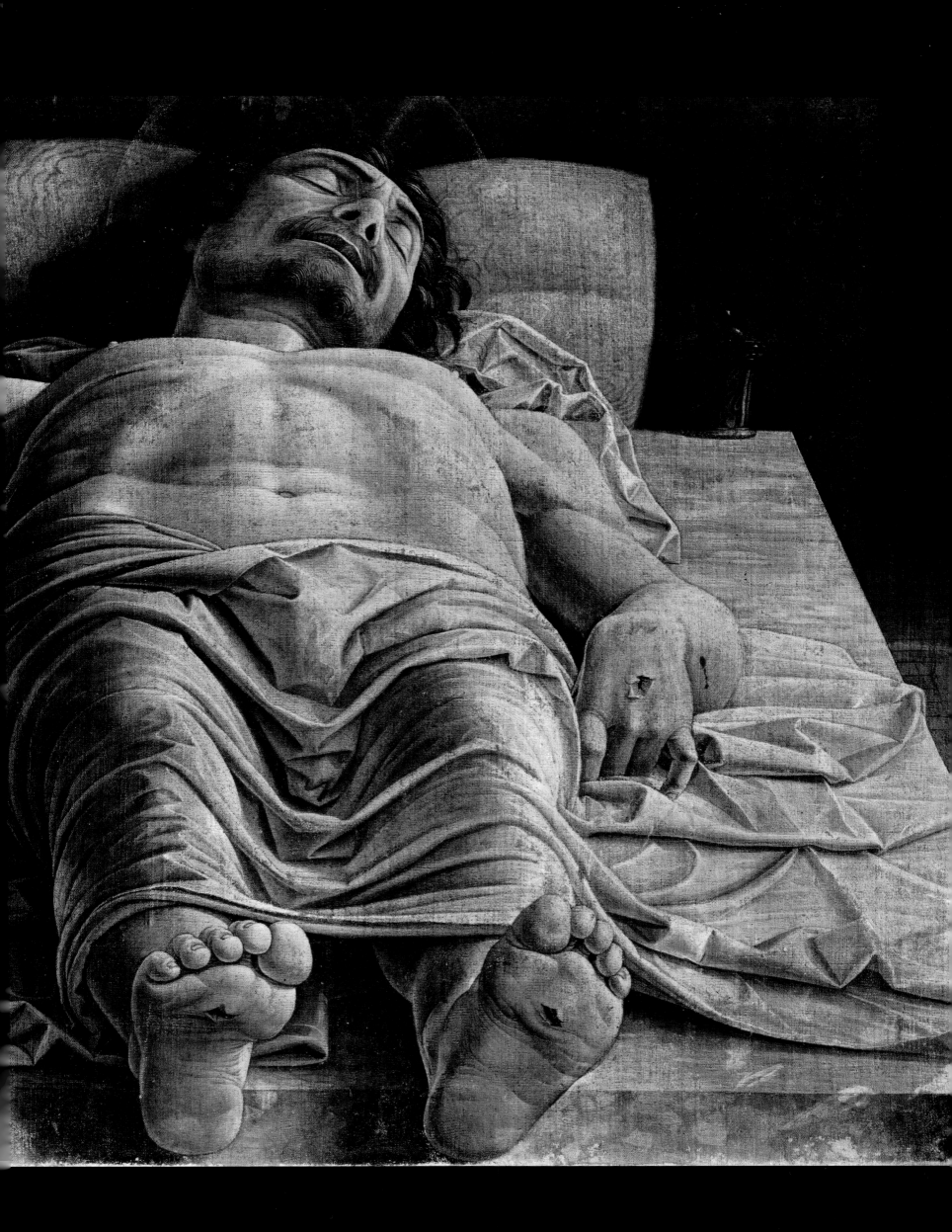

The Holy Sepulcher

292 *The bottomless blackness of the tomb opens disquietingly behind Joseph of Arimathea and Jesus in this* Pietà *by Fra Angelico. A devout man, the master enhanced the innocence of religious themes, often flooding them with clear, soft light that emphasizes the superhuman qualities of the figures.*

293 *The Holy Sepulcher is today housed in an ornate 19th-century building. It was originally part of a rock necropolis just outside Jerusalem's city walls.*

294 *Christ, victorious over death, steps out of the tomb in this illumination taken from an antiphonary by the Florentine Pacino di Buonaguida, who was active in the early 14th century.*

295 *At the end of his painting career, after 1464, Filippo Lippi painted the* Stories of Mary *in the Duomo of Spoleto, from which this balanced, light filled* Death of the Virgin *is taken.*

The ascension of Jesus

Jesus' ascension to Heaven after the Resurrection took place on the other side of the city, on the Mount of Olives that stands beside the road to Bethany. The Ascension is commemorated by two monuments. One is the Church of Eleona ("Olive grove"), which is a basilica built at the instigation of St. Helena over the grotto in which Jesus had predicted the destruction of Jerusalem to his disciples and from which he had left in their company to rise to Heaven. The other is the Imbomon ("Hill"), which is a rotunda open to the sky surrounded by three orders of columns, with flooring made of mosaics and marble. In the center, protected by a metal railing, lay the rock that bore the footprints of Jesus. The Crusaders transformed the triple colonnade into the cells of a monastery. The rock is today enclosed by a chapel and the print of the right foot has been worn away by time. Not far away there used to be a chapel, but it has since disappeared. It had been built on the spot where, according to the apocryphal narratives, Mary met the archangel Gabriel on her way to pray on the Mount of Olives. Gabriel told her that within three days she would be reunited with her Son and gave her a palm leaf as a sign of his triumphal entry into

Paradise. Also according to the Apocrypha, Mary was buried in the Garden of Gethsemane and, on the third day her body was taken up to Heaven. By the 4th century Mary's empty tomb was covered by a basilica and, according to a pilgrim the following century, 250 stone steps led down into the ground to her tomb. The coffin and funerary wrappings left after the Assumption were sent to Constantinople in 451 at the request of Emperor Marcianus and his wife Pulcheria. They were put on display to the public but following this all trace of them was lost. The tomb still has the same appearance that it did in the 5th century, that of a small kiosk with a square base. The Moslems have always respected it and it might be interpreted as a symbol of religious tolerance and sympathy between different faiths. El-Musharraf, one of the first biographers of the Islamic prophet Mohamed, tells that when Mohamed saw Jerusalem during his night flight, there were two lights gleaming on either side of the Temple. "What are those two lights?" he asked the Archangel Gabriel. And Gabriel replied, "The one of the right is the mihrab of your brother David, and the one of the left is the tomb of your sister Mary."

296 and 297 The events in the Gospels, from the
Resurrection of Lazarus to the Assumption of Jesus, are
described in impassioned detail and with skilful use of
perspective and color by Fra Angelico in the Silver Chest.
The final scene is the Lex Amoris (Law of Love) which,
with the Lex Gratiae and Lex Libertatis, compose the
Lex Nova, the instruction offered to the world by the
New Testament.

Index

c = caption

A

Aaron, 87, 96, 106, 112
Abel, 20, 20c, 23, 66
Abia, 144, 170
Abiathar, 157
Abimelech, 63
Abinadab, 143, 151
Abiud, 169c
Abraham, 7, 51c, 52, 52c, 54, 55c,
   57, 57c, 59, 59c, 60, 62c, 63, 65c,
   66, 66c, 68c, 69, 92
Absalom, 152, 153, 157
Abyssinia, 167
Achia, 170
Achilles, 208
Achis, 148
Adam, 5c, 14c, 16, 18, 19, 23, 40,
   46, 66
Adonijah, 157
Adoniram, 170
Adriatic Sea, 199
Aelia Capitolina, 283c
Africa, 125c, 167
Agag, 145, 145c
Agincourt, 223c
Ahab, 125, 171, 172, 177
Ahaziah, 177
Ahio, 151
Akkad, 39
Aladdin, 158
Alexander the Great, 196, 199
Alexandria, 199
Alexas, 208
Amalekites, 131, 144, 145, 145c
Amaziah, 177
Ammon, 60
Amnon, 152
Amon, 184
Amonites, 60, 144, 145
Amorites, 112, 114c, 121, 125c
Amos, 179
Amram, 87
Amurru, 96c
Anagni, 143c
Andrea del Verrocchio, 234c
Andrew, apostle, 240, 241c
Angelo da Messina, 267
Anne, mother of Mary, 211, 276
Antigonus, 206, 208
Antioch, 201
Antiochus III, 199
Antiochus IV Epiphanes, 187c,
   201, 201c

Antipater, 206, 208
Antonino da Piacenza, 245
Apollonius, 201c
Aqaba, Gulf of, 89, 106
Arabs, 131
Aram, 69, 177c
Ararat, Mount, 7, 18, 24, 32c, 33,
   34, 34c, 39
Arasse, 18
Archelaus, 223
Arianna, 9
Aristobulus II, 206
Aristobulus III, 208
Armenia, 24, 33, 34, 34c, 199,
   206
Armenians, 34c
Arnolfo, 66
Artaxerxes I, 196
Ashdod, 131, 140, 143, 143c
Ashqelon, 131, 132, 143
Ashrael, 170
Asia, 196
Assisi, 211c, 214c, 224c, 270c
Assyria, 39, 55c, 182, 188, 195,
   195c
Assyrians, 171
Astarte, 120, 171
Athaliah, 177
Athens, 161
Avignon, 71, 161c
Azor, 169c

B

Baal, 120, 131c, 171, 172, 173c, 182
Baal-Sefon, 100
Baasa, 170
Bab el-Manded, Strait of, 167
Babel, Tower of, 37c, 40c, 43c, 44c,
   46, 46c, 48c
Babylon, 7, 39, 40, 43c, 44c, 52,
   161, 169c, 182, 184, 184c, 187c,
   188, 188c, 191, 193c, 196
Baghdad, 46c
Barak, 129
Barbieri, Giovanni Francesco,
   known as Guercino, 62c
Baris, Mount, 33
Bathsheba, 63, 152, 152c, 153,
   153c
Baybars, 211, 255
Bedford, 24c, 37c
Belbello da Pavia, 20c, 104c
Bellini, Giovanni, 8c
Bel-Marduk, 188, 188c
Belshezzar, 190c, 191
Benadad, 177

Benedict XIII, 201c
Benedictus Arias Montanus, 163c
Beni Hasan, 85c
Benjamin, 81, 144, 170
Bernini, Gian Lorenzo, 138c
Berosus, 33
Berruguete, Pedro, 196c
Berry, Jean de, 57c, 214c, 218c,
   223c, 283c
Bethany, 258, 267, 267c, 270, 275,
   294
Bethel, 129, 170, 171c
Bethesda, 245, 249c
Beth-Hogla, 234
Bethlehem, 134, 145, 145c, 215,
   220, 221c, 223, 227
Bethsaida Giulia, 250
Beth-shan, 148
Beth-shemesh, 143, 143c
Bethshura, 201
Bethulia, 77
Bet-Oron, 201c
Bitter Lakes, 100
Boccaccio, 184c
Bonnat, Léon, 268c
Borghese, Scipione, 138c
Bosch, Hieronymus, 17c
Bossuet, Jacques-Benigne, 16
Botticelli, Sandro, 205c, 215c, 288c,
   304c
Bourg-Achard, 201c
Brera, Pinacoteca di, 8
British Museum, 99c
Bruegel, Jan known as 'Velvet', 59c
Bruegel, Pieter, 'the Elder', 40c, 46c,
   149c
Bubastis, 84
Buonarroti, Michelangelo, 5c
Burgundy, 184c

C

Cades, 129
Caesarea Maritima, 209, 283
Caesarea Philippi, 253, 255
Caiaphas, 276, 278c
Cain, 20, 20c, 23, 66
Cainites, 23
Cairo, 223
Caleb, 112
Caliari Paolo, known as Veronese, 62c
Calmet, Augustin, 163c
Calvary, 283, 286, 286c
Cambridge, 227c
Cana, 240, 245, 245c
Canaan, 39c, 55c, 57, 57c, 71, 71c,
   73c, 77, 81, 81c, 84, 85c, 104,

   106, 112, 113c, 120, 121, 128c,
   129, 131, 140
Canaanites, 39c, 68c
Canterbury, 155c
Capernaum, 240, 240c, 245, 251c,
   253, 258
Caravaggio, Michelangelo Merisi
   known as, 8c, 280c
Cariathiarim, 143, 151c
Carlos II, 132c
Carracci, Annibale, 136c
Caspian Sea, 18
Catalonia, 151c
Catherine, St., 95
Chalanné, 39
Chaldea, 18
Chaldeans, 52
Chamos, 120
Chantilly, 119c
Chison, river, 129
Chosroes, 286
Christ, see Jesus Christ
Cignani, Carlo, 136c
Cleopatra, 125, 208
Constantine, 57, 93c, 95, 220, 257c,
   286
Constantinople, 34, 294
Courcy, Jean de, 43c, 201c
Coypel, Antoine, 68c
Cranach, Lucas, 17c
Crassus, 206
Crete, 131, 134c
Ctesiphon, 39
Cyrenaica, 199
Cyrene, 199
Cyrus, 187c, 191, 193, 193c

D

Dagon, 134, 143, 143c
Daher al-Aziz, 286
Dalmatia, 211
Damascus, 58, 171, 177, 179, 184,
   206
Dan, 170
Daniel, 190c, 191
Daniele da Volterra, 172c
Darius, 193, 196, 196c
David, 7, 119c, 121, 138c, 140c,
   145, 145c, 147c, 148, 150c, 151,
   151c, 152, 152c, 153, 157, 158,
   160, 167, 170, 177, 184, 193, 209,
   211, 215, 270, 294
De Lyre, Nicolas, 160c, 161c
Dead Sea, 60, 61c, 62c, 148, 237,
   238c
Debora, 129, 144

Decker, C., 46
Delacroix, Eugène, 75c, 199c
Delilah, 134, 136c
Des Moulins, Guiard, 99c, 111c, 122c, 140c, 193c
Dome of the Rock, 164c
Doré, Gustave, 32c, 193c
Dothan, 77
Duccio di Buoninsegna, 228c, 245c, 271c, 277c, 278c

E
Ecbatana, 160
Eden, 7, 14c, 16, 17c, 18, 20, 46, 51c, 66
Edom, 112, 182
Edomites, 71, 75c, 112, 144
Edon, 167
Egypt, 7, 57, 76c, 77, 79 81, 81c, 83c, 84, 85, 85c, 87, 89, 89c, 92, 96, 99c, 106, 112, 120, 131, 143, 144, 157, 160, 170, 182, 196, 199, 208, 211, 223, 223c, 255
Ekron, 131
El Azarieh, 267, 268c
El Musharraf, 294
Ela, 145
Elatea, church of, 245
Elath, 167
Eleazarus, 89, 143, 158, 199
Eli, 140, 140c, 143
Eliakim, 169c
Elijah, 172, 172c, 173c, 174c, 175c, 177, 253
Elisha, 172, 175c, 177, 177c
Emmaus, 201
En Gedi, 61c
Endor, 149c
Engebrechtsz, Cornelis, 177c
Enoch, 20, 23
Enochia, 20, 23
Ephraim, 125, 129, 270
Erech, 39
Esau, 68c, 69, 71, 75c
Escha, 227
Esdras, 193c, 196, 196c
Eshtaol, 134
Esther, 195, 195c
Etam, 100, 104
Etemenaki, 188
Ethbaal, 171
Etheria, St., 60
Ethiopia, 167
Eud of Eglon, 128c
Euphrates, 7, 16, 39, 44c, 52, 187c, 188, 191
Eve, 14c, 18, 19, 23, 46, 66
Ezdrelon, plain of, 129
Ezekiel, 169c, 191, 233c
Eziongeber, 167

F
Fetti, Domenico, 91c
Fillastre, Guillaume, 177c, 201c
Fillion, 23
Fischer von Erlach, Johann Bernhard, 188c
Flanders, 196c
Flavius Josephus, 8, 23, 33, 40, 60, 61c, 77, 84, 87, 89, 129, 144, 155c, 158, 167, 187c, 196, 206c, 208, 229, 255, 276
Florence Baptistery, 23c, 81c
Florence, 5c, 52c, 76c, 111c, 169c, 255c
Fouquet, Jean, 155c, 193c, 206c
Fra Angelico, 169c, 231c, 233c, 251c, 255c, 258c, 271c, 275c, 286c, 292c, 296c
Fra' Eustachio, 92c, 111c
Fragonard, Jean-Honoré, 171c
France, 13c, 16, 113c, 119c, 145, 184c, 193c, 223c, 255
France, Jean de, 214c
Frederick II, 255
Ful, 182

G
Gabaa, 125, 157
Gabaa, 144, 145
Gabriel, archangel, 18, 211, 294
Gaddi, Taddeo, 229c
Galaad, 145c, 153
Galilee, 125, 211, 237, 245, 250, 251c, 253, 255
Galilee, Sea of, 234c, 237, 240, 240c, 252c
Galleria Borghese, 138c
Galleria Doria Pamphili, 8c
Gat, 131, 143
Gaulanitide, 253
Gaza, 119c, 131, 134, 196
Gebel el Qafseh, 239
Gebel Harun, 112
Gebel Karantal, 121
Gebel Musa, 6c
Gebel Usdun, 60
Germany, 169c, 184
Gershom, 89
Geshur, 153
Gessen, 84
Gethsemane, 275, 275c, 277c, 294
Gezer, 157
Ghirlandaio, Domenico, 241c
Gideon, 129, 129c, 131, 131c
Gihon, river 16
Gilboa, Mount,131, 148, 149c
Gilgal, 122, 144
Gilgamesh, 30c
Giordano, Luca, 71c, 132c

Giotto, 229c, 267c, 277c
Giovanni di Fiesole, 231c
Giusto de' Menabuoi, 263c
Golgotha, 7, 286, 286c
Goliath, 7, 145
Gomorrah, 59, 61c, 63
Greece, 245
Guercino, 236c

H
Hadassah, 195
Hadrian, 283c, 286
Hagar, 57, 62c, 63
Haggai, 193
Hakem, 286
Hakotel Hama'aravi, 164c
Ham, 37c, 39, 39c, 40c
Haman, 195, 195c
Hamites, 39
Hanukka, 201
Harran, 54, 57c, 68c, 69, 71
Hasmoneans, 201, 206, 208
Hayez, Francesco, 75c
Hazael, 177
Heber, 129
Hebrews (Jews), 75c, 85, 85c, 96c, 114c, 125c, 140c, 164c, 169c, 173c, 184c, 187c, 193c, 195c, 249c, 263c
Hebron, 57, 63, 66, 66c, 69, 129, 148, 151, 153
Helen, St., 93c, 95
Heliodorus, 199
Heliopolis, 81, 84, 223
Herman, 184c
Hermon, Mount, 57, 170, 253, 255
Herod Antipas, 237, 240c, 253
Herod the Great, 125, 206, 208, 209, 209c, 211, 220, 223, 223, 224c, 236c, 237, 240c, 249c, 258c, 260c, 263c, 276, 278c, 286
Herodiad, 237
Herodotus, 188
Hesdin, Jacquemart de, 283c
Hezekiah, 182, 182c, 184c
Hiel of Bethel, 125
Hiram, 151, 160, 167
Hittites, 85, 85c
Hor, 112
Hosea, 179, 179c
Hyksos, 77, 78c, 84
Hyrcanus II, 206
Hyrcanus, 206

I
Iabes, 145c
India, 167
Indus, 18, 199
Iraq, 46c
Isaac, 7, 63, 66, 68c, 69, 75c, 92

Isaiah, 179c, 182c
Ish-bosheth, 151
Ishmael, 57, 62c, 63
Ishmaelites, 77
Ishtar, 188, 188c
Ismail, 66c
Israel, 20c, 75c, 81c, 84, 100c, 104, 104c, 106, 112, 119c, 120, 125, 125c, 129, 131, 134c, 140, 143, 144, 145, 151, 153, 153c, 157, 161, 167, 170, 171, 173c, 177, 179, 182
Israelites, 39c, 83c, 112c, 128c, 131, 131c, 145, 149c, 193c

J
Jabbok, river 71, 73c
Jabesh-Galaad, 148
Jabin, 128c, 129
Jacob, 63, 66, 68c, 69, 71, 71c, 73c, 75c, 76c, 77, 81c, 84, 106, 227
Jacopo del Sellaio, 195c
Jaddo, 196
Jael, 129, 129c
Jaffa, 160
James, 240, 253, 275
Japhet, 39, 39c
Japhethites, 39
Jean Sans Peur, 184c
Jebus, 144, 151
Jeconiah, 169c
Jehu, 177, 177c
Jeremiah, 184, 224c
Jericho, 7, 121, 121c, 122, 122c, 123c, 125, 184, 208, 209, 239
Jeroboam II, 179, 182
Jeroboam, 170, 171, 171c
Jerome, St., 288c
Jerusalem, 7, 63, 66, 125, 129, 144, 151, 153, 155c, 157, 158, 160, 163c, 166c, 169c, 170, 177, 182, 184, 184c, 187c, 188, 191, 193, 193c, 196, 196c, 201, 201c, 206, 206c, 209, 211, 215, 220, 228c, 229, 239, 249c, 258, 258c, 260c, 267, 268c, 270, 272c, 275, 276, 283, 283c, 284c, 285c, 286, 292c, 294
Jesse, 145c
Jesus Christ, 13c, 14c, 33, 52, 172, 215, 215c, 219c, 221c, 223, 227, 227c, 228c, 229, 233c, 234, 234c, 238c, 239, 240, 240c, 245, 245c, 246c, 249c, 250, 251c, 252c, 253, 255, 255c, 257c, 258, 258c, 263c, 267, 267c, 268c, 270, 270c, 271c, 275, 275c, 276, 277c, 278c, 280c, 283, 283c, 286, 288c, 290c, 292c, 294, 294c, 296c, 304c
Jethro, 89, 89c

Jews, 75c, 85, 85c, 96c, 114c, 125c, 140c, 164c, 169c, 173c, 184c, 187c, 193c, 195c, 249c, 263c
Jezebel, 171, 172, 177, 177c
Jezrael, plain of, 129
Joab, 153, 157
Joachim, 211
Joash, 177
Jochabed, 87
Joel, 144
John Chrysostom, St., 34
John the Baptist, 7, 234, 236c, 237, 253, 258
John XXII, 161c
John XXIII, 201c
John, evangelist, 233c, 240, 249c, 253, 275, 288c
Jonah, 7, 125c, 179, 179c
Jonathan, 144, 148, 151
Joram, 177
Jordan, country, 112
Jordan, river, 57, 60, 100c, 112, 119c, 120, 121, 121c, 122, 131, 144, 151, 153, 172, 177, 177c, 184, 234, 234c, 253, 255, 258
Joseph of Arimathaea, 286, 292c
Joseph, Mary's husband, 7, 76c, 77, 78c, 79, 79c, 81, 81c, 84, 215c, 223, 227, 229
Joshua, 7, 112, 119c, 121, 122, 122c, 125, 125c, 128c, 129, 193
Josiah, 184
Jove, 286
Jubal, 23
Judaea, 193, 196, 199, 201, 201c, 206, 208, 209, 215, 223, 267, 278c, 283
Judah, 77, 121, 134, 145, 148, 151, 153, 170, 177, 179, 182, 193, 201, 201c, 227, 238c, 239, 275
Julius Caesar, 206
Justinian, 94c, 95

K

Kadesh-Barnea, 106
Kalné, 39
Kempe, Andrea, 18
Khnumhotep, 85c
Khorsabad, 182
Khovirap Monastery, 34c
Kircher, Athanasius, 24c, 44, 44c, 46
Kiriat Arbat, 66c
Kurà, 18
Kurn Hattin, 250

L

Laban, 69, 71
Labano, 73c
Lamech, 20c, 23

Lazarim, 267
Lazarus, 258, 267, 267c, 270, 296c
Lazarus, Church of, 268c
Le Sueur, Eustache, 246c
Leah, 63, 71, 73c, 77
Lebanon, 151, 158, 160
Leida, 177c
Lenoir, Jean, 283c
Leonardo da Vinci, 211c, 272c
Leonardo di Credi, 234c
Leone, Andrea di, 73c
Levi, 87
Levites, 143c
Lippi, Filippino, 52c, 195c
Lippi, Fra Filippo, 195c, 205c, 294c
Lombardy, 263c
Lorenzetti, Pietro, 270c
Loreto, 211
Lot, 57, 57c, 59, 59c, 61c
Louis IX, St. Louis, king of France, 145, 255
Luke, evangelist, 219c, 228c, 229, 234, 239

M

Maanca, 170
Mabanaim, 151, 206
Macarius, St., 286
Macedonia, 196
Machaerus, fort of, 237
Machpelah, 63, 81, 151
Machpelah, cave of, 66c
Madrid, 132
Magi, kings, 205c, 218c, 220, 220c
Maimonides, 161c
Mainz, 169c
Makkedah, 125, 125c
Malachi, 172
Mamet el-Khalil, 57
Mamre, 57, 63
Manasseh, 131, 182
Manoah, 131
Mantegna, Andrea, 290c
Manzala, lake, 87c
Marches, 211
Marcianus, 294
Mardocheus, 195, 195c
Mariamne, 208
Mark Antony, 206, 208
Mark, evangelist, 252c, 270
Mars, 208
Martha, 258, 270
Martini, Simone, 211
Mary Magdalene, 288c, 304c
Mary, 104, 258, 270
Mary, the Virgin, 5c, 8c, 205c, 211, 211c, 214c, 215c, 220, 221c, 229, 245, 249c, 288c

Mat Khamri, 171
Mattathias, 184, 201, 201c
Matthew, evangelist, 224c, 238c, 258c
Mecca, 24c
Media, 182
Mediterranean Sea, 85, 131, 160, 206
Medzpin, Giacomo di, 34, 52
Megiddo, plain of, 129, 131, 184
Melcha, 227
Melcha, 84
Melek el Kamel, 255
Memphis, 77, 81, 89, 96
Meneptah I, 96
Merisi, Michelangelo, known as Caravaggio, 147c
Merodac-Baladan, 182
Meroes, 89
Mesopotamia, 20, 23, 40c, 52, 55c, 75c
Methuselah, 23
Meuse, 113c
Mexico, 24c
Micah, 172, 179, 179c, 180c
Michael, 112
Michal, 148, 150c, 152, 153c
Michelangelo, 91c, 96c, 172c, 180c
Midian, 89, 89c
Midianites, 89, 89c, 92, 112, 131, 131c
Milan, 8c
Militta, 188
Miniad, 33
Miriam, 87
Mizpeh, 140, 144
Moab, 60, 112, 128c, 148, 182
Moab, Steppes of, 121
Moabites, 60, 112, 144
Modin, 201
Mohamed, 95, 294
Moloch, 120
Moreh, Mount, 131, 148
Moriah, 63, 209
Mortier, Pietre, 100c
Moscow, 114c
Moses, 6c, 7, 83c, 87, 87c, 89, 89c, 91c, 92, 92, 92c, 93c, 94c, 96, 96c, 100, 104, 104c, 106, 109c, 111c, 112, 116c, 120, 253
Mount of Olives, 275, 275c, 294
Mount of the Forty Days (Gebel Karantal), 121, 239
Mount of the Precipice (Gebel el Qafseh), 239
Mount Zion, 272c, 278c
Musée Condé, 119c
Museo del Prado, 132c
Museo dell'Opera del Duomo, 111c

N

Naaman, 177c
Nablus, 75c
Nacas the Ammonite, 145c
Nachon, 151
Nahor, 69
Nahr el Mukatta, 129
Napoleon, 129
Nathan, 152, 153, 153c
Nazareth, 211, 211c, 227, 229, 239, 255, 255c
Near East, 7
Nebo, Mount, 83c, 112, 120
Nebuchadnezzar, 184, 184c, 188c
Necho II, 184
Negev, 106, 112, 112c
Nehemia, 196
New York, 119c
Nicholas Damascene, 33, 208
Nile valley, 77
Nile, river 7, 18, 57, 81, 84, 87, 87c, 89, 96, 99c, 157, 223
Nimrod, 39, 40, 40c, 43c, 44, 48c
Nineveh, 39, 44c, 160, 161, 179, 179c, 182
Ninmach, 188
Nino, 44c
Nisibis, 34
Noah, 7, 24, 24c, 26c, 27c, 30c, 32c, 34c, 37c, 39, 39c, 44, 52
Noema, 23
Normandy, 201c

O

Octavian Augustus, 206, 208, 209
Odysseus, 208
Omar, 63, 260c
Omar's Mosque, 65c
Omri, 171
Ophir, 167
Orchoe, 39
Orvieto, 23c
Oza, 151
Oziah, 179

P

Pacino di Buonaguida, 294c
Paddan-Aram, 54
Padua, 267c
Padua, baptistery, 263c
Palazzo Barberini, 205c
Palestine, 7, 39c, 131, 184, 199, 208, 220, 223c, 239, 286
Palmyra, 57
Pamplona, 19
Paredes de Nava, 196c
Paris, 161c, 184c, 199c
Parmenion, 193
Parthenon, 161
Paul, St., 121

Pentapolis, 59, 60, 62c
Perea, 237, 258, 270
Perin del Vaga, 125c
Persia, 187c, 191, 193, 196, 196c, 218c, 220
Persian Gulf, 18, 52
Peter, apostle, 241c, 250, 253, 270, 271c, 275
Pharan desert, 62c, 63
Pharisees, 246c, 278c
Pharos, island of, 199
Philippe III of France, 109c
Philistia, 182
Philistines, 7, 119c, 131, 132, 134, 134c, 136c, 140, 140c, 143, 143c, 144, 145, 148, 149c
Phoenicia, 182, 253
Piero della Francesca, 166c
Pierpont Morgan Library, 119c
Pison, river 16
Pitom, 85
Poblet, 151c
Polo, Marco, 34
Pompey the Great, 206, 206c
Pontius Pilate, 276, 278c, 283, 304c
Pontus, 206
Potiphar, 76c, 77
Poussin, Nicolas, 114c
Prisse d'Avennes, Emile, 85c
Ptolemy I Soter, 199
Ptolemy II Philadelphus, 199
Ptolemy IV Philopator, 199
Ptolomais, 199
Pulcheria, 294
Pushkin Museum, 114
Pyraeus, 209

Q
Qaaba, 24c

R
Rachel, 71, 73c, 76c, 77, 81, 224c
Raguel, 89, 89c, 92
Rahab, 121, 121c, 122
Raleigh, Walter, 205c
Rama, 129, 144, 145
Ramathainm-Sophim, 144
Ramesseum, 85c, 96c
Ramses II, 85, 85c, 96, 96c, 100, 129
Ramses III, 131
Raphael, 59c, 73c, 92c, 106c, 123c, 125c
Ravenna, 245c
Rebecca, 69
Red Sea, 100, 102c, 121, 167
Reni, Guido, 83c
Resen, 39
Restout, Jean, 73c
Ribera, Jusepe de, 68c
Ribla, 184

Roboamo, 170
Rome, 6c, 8c, 121c, 138c, 205c, 206, 208, 209, 280c
Rosa, Salvator, 65c, 149c
Rosellini, Ippolito, 85cì
Rosso Fiorentino, 91c, 233c
Ruben, 77
Rubens, Peter Paul, 91c, 182c

S
Saint-Sulpice, Church of, 199c
Saladin, 250
Salisbury, 81c
Salome, 206, 208, 236c
Samaria, 171, 172, 177, 179, 182, 258
Samarra, 46c
Samson, 7, 119c, 132, 132c, 134, 134c, 136c, 140
Samuel, 140c, 143, 144, 145, 145c, 148, 149c, 151
San Brizio, Chapel of, 23c
San Francesco, Church of, 211c, 214c, 224c, 270c
San Marco, Monastery of, 255c
San Pietro in Vincoli, 6c
San Salvatore, Church of, 257c
Sant'Apollinare Nuovo, Church of, 245c
Santa Eulalia, Church of, 196c
Santa Maria della Salute, Church of, 147c
Santa Maria Impruneta, Collegiate Church of, 5c
Santa Maria Maggiore, Basilica of, 121
Santa Maria Novella, 52c
Santissima Annunziata, Church of the, 169c, 231c
Sarah, 51c, 57, 57c, 59, 62c, 63, 66c
Sargon II, 182
Satan, 16, 238c, 239
Saul, 144, 145, 145c, 148, 149c, 151, 152
Schedel, Hartmann, 14c
Schiavone, Giorgio, 134c
Schoenfeld, Johann Heinrich, 173c
Scrovegni Chapel, 267c, 277c
Sedom, 61c
Seleucids, 199, 201
Seleucus IV, 199, 201
Semites, 39
Sennaar, 39, 40
Sennacherib, 182
Sermon, Church of the, 251c
Seron, 201c
Sethites, 23
Shealtiel, 169c
Sheba, 7, 166c, 167, 167c
Shem, 39, 39c, 52, 54

Sheshbazzar, 193
Sichem, 75c, 170
Siena, 172c, 228c, 245c, 271c
Signorelli, Luca, 23c, 83c, 116c
Sihon, king, 114c
Siklag, 148
Silo, 125
Simon, 240, 270
Sin, desert, 104, 106
Sinai, 6c, 92, 93c, 95, 104, 106c, 172
Siriada, 23
Sisera, 128c, 129, 129c
Sistine Chapel, 5c, 13c, 18c, 83c, 116c, 172c, 180c, 190c, 241c
Sodom, 57, 59, 59c, 61c, 63, 121
Solomon, 7, 125c, 152c, 153, 153c, 155c, 157, 157c, 158, 160, 160c, 161, 161c, 166c, 167, 167c, 170, 184, 193, 201
Solomon's Temple, 63, 206c, 260c
Sophia of Saxony, 184c
Sorek, 134
Souvigny Bible, 13c, 51c
Souvigny, 157c
Spain, 99c
St. Catherine's Monastery, 93c, 94c
St. Helen, 220, 220c, 255, 257c
St. James, 211
St. Joseph, 211
St. Luke, 211
St. Mark's Basilica, 27c, 39c, 57c, 78c, 79c, 89c, 150c, 179c, 252c
St. Petersburg, 193c
Strozzi, Bernardo, 241c
Succot, 100
Suez Canal, 100
Suez, Gulf of, 104
Suleiman the Magnificent, 270
Sumerians, 52
Sur, desert, 104
Surikov, Vasily, 190c
Syria, 23, 55c, 184, 196, 199, 201c, 206, 208

T
Tabgha, 251c, 252c
Tabor, 129, 255, 255c
Tadmor, 57
Tamar, 152
Tamath Lekhi, 134
Tamnat-Sareh, 125
Tanis, 84, 85
Tarbi, 89
Tecamchalco, 24c
Tell-el-Ful, 144
Tempesta, Antonio, 102c
Temptation, Mount of the, 238c
Terah, 52, 54
Terebinth, Valley of the, 145
Tersatto, 211

Thebes, 161
Theodoric, 234
Tiberias, 237, 240c
Tiberias, Lake, 234c, 240, 250
Tiberius, 234
Tiglathpileser III, 182
Tigris, river 16, 39, 44c, 182
Timnath, 131
Timsah, Lake, 85
Tintoretto, 134c
Tissot, James, 209c
Titian, 286
Titus, 263c
Tommaso di Baldassare, 111c
Tubalcain, 23
Tyre, 151, 160, 167, 171, 196, 253

U
Uadi es-Samt, 145
Uffizi, Museo degli, 5c, 211c
Ur, 52, 52c, 54
Urfa, 52
Uriah, 152
Ur-Nammu, 52c
Ut-napishtim, 30c

V
Vaccaro, Andrea, 68c
Van Eyck, Hubert, 180c
Van Eyck, Jan, 180c
Van Lint, Pieter, 249c
Vasselin, family, 152c
Vatican City, 5c
Venice, 27c, 39c, 57c, 78c, 89c, 147c, 150c, 179c, 252c, 257c
Versailles, 46
Vespasian, 158
Vienna, National Library of, 13c
Vinci, Leonardo da, 5c
Voltaire, 46

W
Warka, 39
Westminster, 138c
Woolley, Sir Leonard, 52
Wurzburg, John of, 283
Xerxes I, 195, 196

Y
Yaakov, Abraham bar, 125c
Yzreel, valley of, 255c

Z
Zaccariah, 193
Zadok, 169c
Zedekiah, 184
Zerubbabel, 169c, 193, 209
Zeus, 201
Zion, 151, 193, 270, 283
Zipporah, 89, 94c

Photographic Credits

Page 1 Archivio Scala
Pages 2-3 Musei Vaticani
Pages 4-5 Giovanni Dagli Orti
Page 6 Araldo De Luca
Page 7 Antonio Attini/Archivio White Star
Page 8 Araldo De Luca
Page 9 Archivio Scala
Pages 10-11 Musei Vaticani
Page 12 Eric Lessing Culture and Fine Arts Archives/Contrasto
Page 13 Eric Lessing Culture and Fine Arts Archives/Contrasto
Page 14 top right Archivio Storico Il Dagherrotipo
Page 14 top left Archivio Storico Il Dagherrotipo
Page 14 center right Archivio Storico Il Dagherrotipo
Page 14 center left Archivio Storico Il Dagherrotipo
Page 14 bottom right Archivio Storico Il Dagherrotipo
Page 14 bottom left Archivio Storico Il Dagherrotipo
Page 15 top Historical Picture Archive/Corbis/Contrasto
Page 15 bottom Archivio Storico Il Dagherrotipo
Page 16 Francis G. Mayer/Corbis/Contrasto
Pages 16-17 Francis G. Mayer/Corbis/Contrasto
Page 18-19 Musei Vaticani
Page 20 top Geoffrey Clements/Corbis/Contrasto
Page 20 bottom Archivio Scala
Page 20-21 Eric Lessing Culture and Fine Arts Archives/Contrasto
Page 22 Archivio Scala
Page 23 Archivio Scala
Page 24 top AISA
Page 24 bottom left Topham Picturepoint/Double's/ICP
Page 24 bottom right The Art Archive
Page 25 Giovanni Dagli Orti
Page 26-27 Staatsbibliothek Bamberg, Bamberg, Germany
Page 28 Cameraphoto
Page 29 top Eric Lessing Culture and Fine Arts Archives/Contrasto
Page 29 bottom Eric Lessing Culture and Fine Arts Archives/Contrasto
Page 30 top Topham Picturepoint/Double's/ICP
Page 30 center left Topham Picturepoint/Double's/ICP
Page 30 center right Topham Picturepoint/Double's/ICP
Page 30 bottom left Topham Picturepoint/Double's/ICP
Page 30 bottom right Topham Picturepoint/Double's/ICP
Page 31 Giovanni Dagli Orti
Pages 32-33 Reza/Webistan/Corbis/Contrasto
Page 33 Bettmann/Corbis/Contrasto
Page 34 AISA
Page 35 Gaillarde Raphael/Gamma/Contrasto
Page 36 Topham Picturepoint/Double's/ICP
Page 37 The Art Archive
Page 38-39 Giovanni Dagli Orti
Page 40-41 Giovanni Dagli Orti
Page 42 Archivio Scala
Page 43 left Topham Picturepoint/Double's/ICP
Page 43 right Archivio Scala

Page 44 left Bibliothèque Nationale de France, Paris
Page 44 right Bibliothèque Nationale de France, Paris
Page 45 Bibliothèque Nationale de France, Paris
Page 46 Henry e Anne Stierlin
Page 47 Biblioteca Nazionale Marciana, Venezia
Page 48 Archivio Scala
Pages 48-49 Archivio Scala
Page 50 Eric Lessing Culture and Fine Arts Archives/Contrasto
Page 51 Eric Lessing Culture and Fine Arts Archives/Contrasto
Page 52 Archivio Scala
Page 53 Nik Wheeler/Corbis/Contrasto
Page 54 top AISA
Page 54 bottom Dean Conger/Corbis/Contrasto
Pages 54-55 Dean Conger/Corbis/Contrasto
Pages 56-57 Archivio Scala
Page 56 bottom Archivio Scala
Page 57 Bibliothèque Nationale de France, Paris
Pages 58-59 Archivio Scala
Page 59 Arthotek
Page 60 top Ricki Rosen/Corbis Saba/Contrasto
Page 60 bottom Eric Lessing Culture and Fine Arts Archives/Contrasto
Pages 60-61 Radu Mendrea
Page 62 Eric Lessing Culture and Fine Arts Archives/Contrasto
Pages 62-63 AISA
Page 64 Christie's Images/Corbis/Contrasto
Page 65 Marcello Bertinetti/Archivio White Star
Page 66 top Dean Conger/Corbis/Contrasto
Page 66 bottom Elisabeth Gilbert/Radu Mendrea
Page 67 Dean Conger/Corbis/Contrasto
Page 68 Eric Lessing Culture and Fine Arts Archives/Contrasto
Page 69 top Archivio Scala
Page 69 bottom The Art Archive
Page 70 Eric Lessing Culture and Fine Arts Archives/Contrasto
Page 71 The Art Archive
Page 72 Eric Lessing Culture and Fine Arts Archives/Contrasto
Page 73 top The Art Archive
Page 73 center Archivio Scala
Page 73 bottom Eric Lessing Culture and Fine Arts Archives/Contrasto
Page 74 Eric Lessing Culture and Fine Arts Archives/Contrasto
Page 75 top Giovanni Dagli Orti
Page 75 bottom Eric Lessing Culture and Fine Arts Archives/Contrasto
Pages 76-77 top Eric Lessing Culture and Fine Arts Archives/Contrasto
Pages 76-77 bottom Eric Lessing Culture and Fine Arts Archives/Contrasto
Page 78 top Archivio Scala
Page 78 bottom Archivio Scala
Page 79 top Archivio Scala
Page 79 center left Archivio Scala
Page 79 center right Archivio Scala
Page 80 The Bodleian Library/The Art Archive
Page 81 top Archivio Scala
Page 81 bottom Eric Lessing Culture and Fine Arts Archives/Contrasto

Page 82 Giovanni Dagli Orti
Page 83 Archivio Scala
Page 84 top Archivio White Star
Page 84 bottom Archivio White Star
Page 85 top Archivio White Star
Page 85 bottom Archivio White Star
Page 86 Marcello Bertinetti/ Archivio White Star
Page 87 Archivio Scala
Page 88 top Archivio Scala
Page 88 bottom left Archivio Scala
Page 88 bottom right Archivio Scala
Page 89 left Archivio Scala
Page 89 right Archivio Scala
Page 90 Lessing Archive /Contrasto
Page 91 Eric Lessing Culture and Fine Arts Archives/Contrasto
Page 92 top Archivio Scala
Page 92 bottom Archivio Scala
Page 93 top Antonio Attini/Archivio White Star
Page 93 bottom Marwan Naamani-STF/AFP/ De Bellis
Page 94-95 Marcello Bertinetti/ Archivio White Star
Page 95 Antonio Attini/Archivio White Star
Page 96 Archivio White Star
Page 97 Araldo De Luca
Page 98 Bibliothèque Nationale de France, Paris
Page 99 top The Art Archive
Page 99 bottom left The Bridgeman Art Library
Page 99 bottom right The Bridgeman Art Library
Page 100 Bibliothèque Nationale de France, Paris
Pages 100-101 Archivio White Star
Page 102 Archivio Scala
Pages 102-103 Antonio Attini/Archivio White Star
Page 104 Archivio Scala
Page 105 Giovanni Dagli Orti
Page 106 Archivio Scala
Page 107 Marcello Bertinetti/Archivio White Star
Pages 108-109 Topham Picturepoint/ Double's/ICP
Page 109 Topham Picturepoint/Double's/ICP
Page 110 Archivio Scala
Page 111 The Art Archive
Page 112 top Itamar Grinberg/Archivio White Star
Page 112 bottom The Bridgeman Art Library
Pages 112-113 Itamar Grinberg/Archivio White Star
Pages 114-115 Eric Lessing Culture and Fine Arts Archives/Contrasto
Pages 116-117 Archivio Scala
Page 118 The Bridgeman Art Library
Page 119 The Bridgeman Art Library
Pages 120-121 Archivio Scala
Page 121 Archivio Scala
Page 122 Bibliothèque Nationale de France, Paris
Pages 122-123 Archivio Scala
Page 124 Archivio Scala
Page 125 Archivio Scala
Page 126/127 The Eran Laor Collection/The Jewish National & University Library, Jerusalem
Page 128 Archivio Scala

Page 129 Archivio Scala
Page 130 Archivio Scala
Page 131 Topham Picturepoint/Double's/ICP
Pages 132-133 Archivio Scala
Page 134 The Bridgeman Art Library
Page 135 The Bridgeman Art Library
Page 136 Archivio Scala
Page 137 Archivio Scala
Page 138 The Art Archive
Page 139 Araldo De Luca
Page 140 The Art Archive
Page 141 Archivio Scala
Page 142 Archivio Scala
Page 143 top left The Art Archive
Page 143 top right The Art Archive
Page 143 bottom The Art Archive
Page 144 top Archivio Scala
Page 144 bottom Archivio Scala
Page 145 top Archivio Scala
Page 145 bottom Archivio Scala
Pages 146-147 Eric Lessing Culture and Fine Arts Archives/Contrasto
Page 147 Eric Lessing Culture and Fine Arts Archives/Contrasto
Page 148 Eric Lessing Culture and Fine Arts Archives/Contrasto
Pages 148-149 Aly Meyer/Corbis/Contrasto
Page 150 Archivio Scala
Page 151 top Archivio Scala
Page 151 center Bibliothèque Nationale de France, Paris
Page 151 bottom Bibliothèque Nationale de France, Paris
Page 152 Topham Picturepoint/Double's/ICP
Pages 152-153 Giovanni Dagli Orti
Page 153 Bibliothèque Nationale de France, Paris
Page 154 The Bridgeman Art Library
Page 155 Archivio Scala
Pages 156-157 Giovanni Dagli Orti
Page 157 Bibliothèque Nationale de France, Paris
Page 158 Archivio Scala
Page 159 Archivio Scala
Page 160 Photo 12
Page 161 top Photo 12
Page 161 bottom left Topham Picturepoint/Double's/ICP
Page 161 bottom right The Art Archive
Pages 162-163 Giovanni Dagli Orti
Page 163 Bojan Brecelj/Corbis/Contrasto
Page 164 M. Bertinetti/Archivio White Star
Page 165 Antonio Attini/Archivio White Star
Pages 166-167 Archivio Scala
Page 167 The Bridgeman Art Library
Page 168 Archivio Scala
Page 169 Eric Lessing Culture and Fine Arts Archives/Contrasto
Page 170-171 Eric Lessing Culture and Fine Arts Archives/Contrasto
Page 172 Archivio Scala
Pages 172-173 Eric Lessing Culture and Fine Arts Archives/Contrasto
Page 174 The Art Archive
Page 175 Eric Lessing Culture and Fine Arts Archives/Contrasto
Page 176 Bibliothèque Nationale de France, Paris
Page 177 Eric Lessing Culture and Fine Arts Archives/Contrasto
Page 178-179 Giovanni Dagli Orti
Page 179 left Archivio Scala
Page 179 center Archivio Scala
Page 179 right Archivio Scala
Page 180 AISA
Page 181 Eric Lessing Culture and Fine Arts Archives/Contrasto

Pages 182-183 Eric Lessing Culture and Fine Arts Archives/Contrasto
Pages 184-185 Eric Lessing Culture and Fine Arts Archives/Contrasto
Page 184 Eric Lessing Culture and Fine Arts Archives/Contrasto
Page 185 The Art Archive
Page 186 Giovanni Dagli Orti
Page 187 Mary Evans Picture Library
Pages 188-189 Historical Picture Archive/Corbis/Contrasto
Page 188 Giovanni Dagli Orti
Page 189 Henri Stierlin
Page 190-191 Archivio Scala
Page 191 Eric Lessing Culture and Fine Arts Archives/Contrasto
Page 192 Eric Lessing Culture and Fine Arts Archives/Contrasto
Page 193 top Mary Evans Picture Library
Page 193 bottom Mary Evans Picture Library
Pages 194-195 Eric Lessing Culture and Fine Arts Archives/Contrasto
Page 195 Eric Lessing Culture and Fine Arts Archives/Contrasto
Page 196 Archivio Scala
Page 197 The Art Archive
Pages 198-199 Eric Lessing Culture and Fine Arts Archives/Contrasto
Pages 200-201 Archivio Scala
Page 201 Bibliothèque Nationale de France, Paris
Pages 202-203 Eric Lessing Culture and Fine Arts Archives/Contrasto
Page 204 Double's/ICP
Page 205 The Art Archive
Page 207 The Bridgeman Art Library
Page 209 The Bridgeman Art Library
Pages 210-211 Eric Lessing Culture and Fine Arts Archives/Contrasto
Page 210 Marcello Bertinetti/Archivio White Star
Pages 212-213 Elio Ciol/Corbis/Contrasto
Pages 214-215 Elio Ciol/Corbis/Contrasto
Page 216 Roger Viollet Collection/ Archivi Alinari
Page 217-218 Burstein Collection/Corbis/Contrasto
Page 218 Bibliothèque Nationale de France, Paris
Page 219 Bibliothèque Nationale de France, Paris
Page 220 Antonio Attini/Archivio White Star
Page 220-221 Eric Lessing Culture and Fine Arts Archives/Contrasto
Page 222 Bibliothèque Nationale de France, Paris
Page 223 The Bridgeman Art Library
Page 224 Archivio Scala
Pages 224-225 Elio Ciol/Corbis/Contrasto
Page 226 The Bridgeman Art Library
Page 227 The Bridgeman Art Library
Pages 228-229 Archivio Scala
Page 229 Archivio Scala
Pages 230-231 Archivio Scala
Page 232 Archivio Scala
Page 233 Archivio Scala
Page 234 Itamar Grinberg/Archivio White Star
Pages 234-235 Eric Lessing Culture and Fine Arts Archives/Contrasto
Pages 236-237 Giovanni Dagli Orti
Pages 238-239 Eric Lessing Culture and Fine Arts Archives/Contrasto
Page 239 top Topham Picturepoint/Double's/ICP
Page 239 bottom Eric Lessing Culture and Fine Arts Archives/Contrasto
Page 240 Itamar Grinberg/Archivio White Star

Pages 240-241 Archivio Scala
Pages 241-242 Arte & Immagini srl/Corbis/Contrasto
Pages 244-245 Giovanni Dagli Orti
Page 245 Archivio Scala
Page 246 Eric Lessing Culture and Fine Arts Archives/Contrasto
Page 247 Eric Lessing Culture and Fine Arts Archives/Contrasto
Pages 248-249 Eric Lessing Culture and Fine Arts Archives/Contrasto
Page 250 Archivio Scala
Pages 250-251 Itamar Grinberg/Archivio White Star
Pages 252-253 Archivio Scala
Page 252 Antonio Attini/Archivio White Star
Page 254 Itamar Grinberg/Archivio White Star
Page 255 Archivio Scala
Pages 256-257 Archivio Scala
Page 257 Itamar Grinberg
Page 258 Archivio Scala
Pages 258-259 Archivio Scala
Pages 260-261 Marcello Bertinetti/Archivio White Star
Pages 262-263 Archivio Scala
Pages 264-265 Itamar Grinberg/Archivio White Star
Page 266-267 Giovanni Dagli Orti
Page 267 Garo Nalbandian/Israel Images
Page 268 Richard T. Nowitz/Corbis/Contrasto
Pages 268-269 Giovanni Dagli Orti
Page 270 Archivo Iconografico, S.A./Corbis/Contrasto
Page 271 top Topham Picturepoint/Double's/ICP
Page 271 bottom Archivio Scala
Page 272 Antonio Attini/Archivio White Star
Pages 272-273 Ghigo Roli
Page 274 Itamar Grinberg/Archivio White Star
Page 275 Archivio Scala
Page 276 Giovanni Dagli Orti
Page 277 Giovanni Dagli Orti
Page 278 top left Archivio Scala
Page 278 top right Archivio Scala
Page 278 bottom left Archivio Scala
Page 278 bottom right Archivio Scala
Page 279 top Archivio Scala
Page 279 bottom Archivio Scala
Page 280 Giovanni Dagli Orti
Pages 280-281 Giovanni Dagli Orti
Page 282 top Bibliothèque Nationale de France, Paris
Page 282 bottom left Bibliothèque Nationale de France, Paris
Page 282 bottom right Bibliothèque Nationale de France, Paris
Page 283 left Bibliothèque Nationale de France, Paris
Page 283 right Bibliothèque Nationale de France, Paris
Page 284 Koren Ziv/Gamma/Contrasto
Pages 284-285 Gyori Antoine/Corbis Sygma/Contrasto
Page 286 Antonio Attini/Archivio White Star
Pages 286-287 Archivio Scala
Pages 288-289 Eric Lessing Culture and Fine Arts Archives/Contrasto
Page 290 Antonio Attini /Archivio White Star
Pages 290-291 Archivio Scala
Page 292 Archivio Scala
Page 293 Antonio Attini/Archivio White Star
Page 294 Archivio Scala
Pages 294-295 Archivio Scala
Page 296 Archivio Scala
Page 297 Archivio Scala
Page 304 Eric Lessing Culture and Fine Arts Archives/Contrasto

304 *Mary Magdalene brings her face close to that of the Messiah in the* The Dead Christ Mourned, *painted by Botticelli, between 1490 and 1492. It is not easy to pinpoint the date of the death of Jesus: according to the Gospels it took place during the office of Pontius Pilate, who was dismissed in AD 36, accused of corruption. It is possible that the year was AD 33, when Jesus would have been between 35 and 40 years of age.*